Writing 1

Meredith Pike-Baky

Heinle & Heinle
Thomson Learning™

Australia • Canada • Denmark • Japan • Mexico
New Zealand • Philippines • Puerto Rico • Singapore
Spain • United Kingdom • United States

Developmental Editors: Jennifer Monaghan, Jill Korey O'Sullivan
Sr. Production Coordinator: Maryellen E. Killeen
Market Development Director: Charlotte Sturdy
Sr. Manufacturing Coordinator: Mary Beth Hennebury
Interior Design: Julia Gecha
Illustrations: Pre-Press Company, Inc., Antonio Castro
Photo Research: Martha Friedman

Cover Design: Ha Nguyen Design
Cover Images: PhotoDisc®
Composition/Production: Pre-Press Company, Inc.
Freelance Production Editor: Janet McCartney
Copyeditor: Donald Pharr
Printer/Binder: Bawden

For permission to use material from this text, contact us:
web   www.thomsonrights.com
fax   1-800-730-2215
phone   1-800-730-2214

For photo credits, see page 205.

Heinle & Heinle Publishers
20 Park Plaza
Boston, MA 02116

UK/EUROPE/MIDDLE EAST:
Thomson Learning
Berkshire House
168-173 High Holborn
London, WC1V 7AA, United Kingdom

AUSTRALIA/NEW ZEALAND:
Nelson/Thomson Learning
102 Dodds Street
South Melbourne
Victoria 3205 Australia

CANADA:
Nelson/Thomson Learning
1120 Birchmount Road
Scarborough, Ontario
Canada M1K 5G4

LATIN AMERICA:
Thomson Learning
Seneca, 53
Colonia Polanco
11560 México D.F. México

ASIA (excluding Japan):
Thomson Learning
60 Albert Street #15-01
Albert Complex
Singapore 189969

JAPAN:
Thomson Learning
Palaceside Building, 5F
1-1-1 Hitotsubashi, Chiyoda-ku
Tokyo 100 0003, Japan

SPAIN:
Thomson Learning
Calle Magallanes, 25
28015-Madrid
España

Library of Congress Cataloging-in-Publication Data
Pike-Baky, Meredith,
    Tapestry writing 1 / Meredith Pike-Baky.
        p. cm.
    ISBN 0-8384-0033-7 (alk. paper)
    1. English language—Textbooks for foreign speakers. 2. English
language—Rhetoric—Problems, exercises, etc. 3. Report writing—Problems, exercises,
etc. I. Title: Tapestry writing one. II. Title.

PE1128 .P515 2000
808'.042—dc21   99-057626

 This book is printed on acid-free recycled paper.

Printed in the United States of America.
1 2 3 4 5 6 7 8 9 03 02 01 00 99

A VERY SPECIAL THANK YOU

The publisher and authors would like to thank the following coordinators and instructors who have offered many helpful insights and suggestions for change throughout the development of the new *Tapestry*.

Alicia Aguirre, *Cañada College*
Fred Allen, *Mission College*
Maya Alvarez-Galvan, *University of Southern California*
Geraldine Arbach, *Collège de l'Outaouais, Canada*
Dolores Avila, *Pasadena City College*
Sarah Bain, *Eastern Washington University*
Kate Baldus, *San Francisco State University*
Fe Baran, *Chabot College*
Gail Barta, *West Valley College*
Karen Bauman, *Biola University*
Liza Becker, *Mt. San Antonio College*
Leslie Biaggi, *Miami-Dade Community College*
Andrzej Bojarczak, *Pasadena City College*
Nancy Boyer, *Golden West College*
Glenda Bro, *Mt. San Antonio College*
Brooke Brummitt, *Palomar College*
Linda Caputo, *California State University, Fresno*
Alyce Campbell, *Mt. San Antonio College*
Barbara Campbell, *State University of New York, Buffalo*
Robin Carlson, *Cañada College*
Ellen Clegg, *Chapman College*
Karin Cintron, *Aspect ILS*
Diane Colvin, *Orange Coast College*
Martha Compton, *University of California, Irvine*
Nora Dawkins, *Miami-Dade Community College*
Beth Erickson, *University of California, Davis*
Charles Estus, *Eastern Michigan University*
Gail Feinstein Forman, *San Diego City College*
Jeffra Flaitz, *University of South Florida*
Kathleen Flynn, *Glendale Community College*
Ann Fontanella, *City College of San Francisco*
Sally Gearhart, *Santa Rosa Junior College*
Alice Gosak, *San José City College*
Kristina Grey, *Northern Virginia Community College*
Tammy Guy, *University of Washington*
Gail Hamilton, *Hunter College*
Patty Heiser, *University of Washington*
Virginia Heringer, *Pasadena City College*

Catherine Hirsch, *Mt. San Antonio College*
Helen Huntley, *West Virginia University*
Nina Ito, *California State University, Long Beach*
Patricia Jody, *University of South Florida*
Diana Jones, *Angloamericano, Mexico*
Loretta Joseph, *Irvine Valley College*
Christine Kawamura, *California State University, Long Beach*
Gregory Keech, *City College of San Francisco*
Kathleen Keesler, *Orange Coast College*
Daryl Kinney, *Los Angeles City College*
Maria Lerma, *Orange Coast College*
Mary March, *San José State University*
Heather McIntosh, *University of British Columbia, Canada*
Myra Medina, *Miami-Dade Community College*
Elizabeth Mejia, *Washington State University*
Cristi Mitchell, *Miami-Dade Community College*
Sylvette Morin, *Orange Coast College*
Blanca Moss, *El Paso Community College*
Karen O'Neill, *San José State University*
Bjarne Nielsen, *Central Piedmont Community College*
Katy Ordon, *Mission College*
Luis Quesada, *Miami-Dade Community College*
Gustavo Ramírez Toledo, *Colegio Cristóbol Colón, Mexico*
Nuha Salibi, *Orange Coast College*
Alice Savage, *North Harris College*
Dawn Schmid, *California State University, San Marcos*
Mary Kay Seales, *University of Washington*
Denise Selleck, *City College of San Francisco*
Gail Slater, *Brooklyn and Staten Island Superintendency*
Susanne Spangler, *East Los Angeles College*
Karen Stanley, *Central Piedmont Community College*
Sara Storm, *Orange Coast College*
Margaret Teske, *ELS Language Centers*
Maria Vargas-O'Neel, *Miami-Dade Community College*
James Wilson, *Mt. San Antonio College and Pasadena City College*
Karen Yoshihara, *Foothill College*

ACKNOWLEDGMENTS

Thanks to Erik Gundersen, whose encouragement and support made it happen, Jennifer Monaghan, whose sensitive and skillful adoption of the project made it better, and Helen Kalkstein and June McKay, whose careful reading and responding made it relevant to student needs.

Tapestry Writing 1: Contents

ACADEMIC POWER STRATEGIES	**CNN VIDEO CLIPS**	**GRAMMAR YOU CAN USE**	**FROM READING TO WRITING**
Create a Writer's Portfolio to keep track of your learning.	"Kan's Dream for Success" A Vietnamese immigrant in the United States has an unusual dream for success.	Past and present tense verbs	Reading 1: a newspaper article about an immigrant's success in the United States Reading 2: an article about a man overcoming a difficult challenge **Writing Activity:** A story about a person who you consider to be successful
Set goals in order to focus your learning.	"Feng Shui Around the World" People look for places to live that bring harmony and success to their lives	Countable and noncountable nouns	Reading 1: an excerpt from a news article about a special recreation room in a hospital Reading 2: a news article about the ancient Chinese art of Feng Shui **Writing Activity:** A description of a place that has an affect on you
Be an active learner to learn and remember more.	"Online Grandpa" A senior citizen spends his time learning new skills.	Capital letters	Reading 1: a list of tips for healthy aging Reading 2: a story about a senior who rode in a difficult bicycle race **Writing Activity:** A paragraph about an active senior you know
Learn about the library to gather information for your writing.	"What's So Special About Las Vegas?" You can visit many smaller cities in this big city!	Prepositions	Reading 1: a description of a park in San Francisco, California Reading 2: a description of a casino in Las Vegas, Nevada **Writing Activity:** A description of a place to visit
Learn about cultural differences in order to appreciate where you are living and where your classmates come from.	"Superteen" The story of a teenager who knows more than most adults.	Past habitual tense	Reading 1: an article about a teenager from New York City Reading 2: an article about modern teenagers **Writing Activity:** A paragraph about a teenager you know

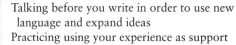

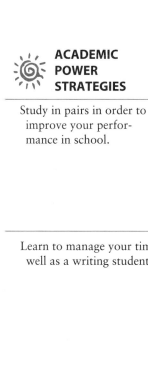 ACADEMIC POWER STRATEGIES	CNN VIDEO CLIPS	GRAMMAR YOU CAN USE	FROM READING TO WRITING
Study in pairs in order to improve your performance in school.	"Love Doctor" A popular expert on relationships between men and women gives advice.	Cause-result sentences	Reading 1: a letter from an advice column about friendship Reading 2: a legend about two friends **Writing Activity:** A paragraph about how to make a friendship strong
Learn to manage your time well as a writing student.	"Letting Go" How some parents in the United States feel about saying goodbye to their children when they go away to college.	Personal pronouns	Reading 1: a son's story of his difficult relationship with his father Reading 2: a story about how the writer's mother came to America to start a new life **Writing Activity:** A short essay about your mother or father or someone who acted like a parent to you
Use a computer when you write.	"Tough Teen Driving Laws" Strict rules for teenage drivers may prevent automobile accidents.	Expressions of obligation	Reading 1: an excerpt from a booklet on driving safely Reading 2: an article about the steps to getting a driver's license **Writing Activity:** A short essay about cars or driving
Learn to appreciate the differences among people in order to succeed in a diverse world.	"Type D Personality" There is information about a new personality type everyone should know.	Word parts	Reading 1: an article about the Enneagram, a system of personality types Reading 2: a chart describing the personality types in the Enneagram **Writing Activity:** A paragraph about your personality type
Reflect on what you've learned so that you can recognize your accomplishments.	"High-Tech Gadgets" We can buy lighter, cheaper, more convenient machines every year.	Passive voice	Reading 1: an article about the invention of ice cream cones Reading 2: a passage about how the use of guide dogs for the blind began **Writing Activity:** Two or more paragraphs about an invention

Welcome to TAPESTRY!

Empower your students with the Tapestry Writing series!

Language learning can be seen as an ever-developing tapestry woven with many threads and colors. The elements of the tapestry are related to different language skills such as listening and speaking, reading, and writing; the characteristics of the teachers; the desires, needs, and backgrounds of the students; and the general second language development process. When all of these elements are working together harmoniously, the result is a colorful, continuously growing tapestry of language competence of which the student and the teacher can be proud.

Tapestry is built upon a framework of concepts that helps students become proficient in English and prepared for the academic and social challenges in college and beyond. The following principles underlie the instruction provided in all of the components of the **Tapestry** program:

◈ Empowering students to be responsible for their learning

◈ Using Language Learning Strategies and Academic Power Strategies to enhance one's learning, both in and out of the classroom

◈ Offering motivating activities that recognize a variety of learning styles

◈ Providing authentic and meaningful input to heighten learning and communication

◈ Learning to understand and value different cultures

◈ Integrating language skills to increase communicative competence

◈ Providing goals and ongoing self-assessment to monitor progress

Guide to Tapestry Writing

Setting Goals focuses students' attention on the learning they will do in each chapter.

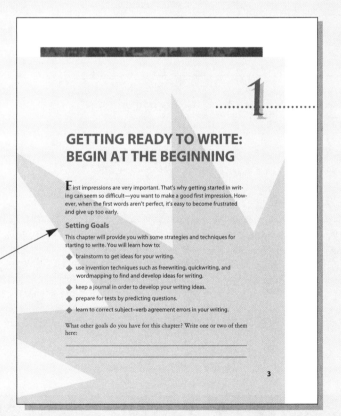

1

GETTING READY TO WRITE: BEGIN AT THE BEGINNING

First impressions are very important. That's why getting started in writing can seem so difficult—you want to make a good first impression. However, when the first words aren't perfect, it's easy to become frustrated and give up too early.

Setting Goals

This chapter will provide you with some strategies and techniques for starting to write. You will learn how to:

◈ brainstorm to get ideas for your writing.

◈ use invention techniques such as freewriting, quickwriting, and wordmapping to find and develop ideas for writing.

◈ keep a journal in order to develop your writing ideas.

◈ prepare for tests by predicting questions.

◈ learn to correct subject–verb agreement errors in your writing.

What other goals do you have for this chapter? Write one or two of them here:

_____

_____

3

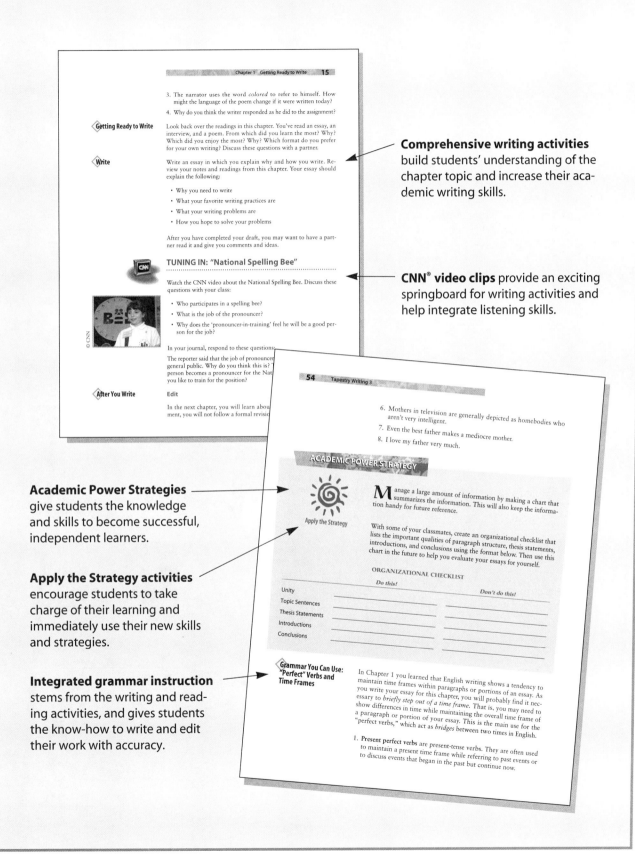

3. The narrator uses the word *colored* to refer to himself. How might the language of the poem change if it were written today?

4. Why do you think the writer responded as he did to the assignment?

Getting Ready to Write

Look back over the readings in this chapter. You've read an essay, an interview, and a poem. From which did you learn the most? Why? Which did you enjoy the most? Why? Which format do you prefer for your own writing? Discuss these questions with a partner.

Write

Write an essay in which you explain why and how you write. Review your notes and readings from this chapter. Your essay should explain the following:

- Why you need to write
- What your favorite writing practices are
- What your writing problems are
- How you hope to solve your problems

After you have completed your draft, you may want to have a partner read it and give you comments and ideas.

TUNING IN: "National Spelling Bee"

Watch the CNN video about the National Spelling Bee. Discuss these questions with your class:

- Who participates in a spelling bee?
- What is the job of the pronouncer?
- Why does the 'pronouncer-in-training' feel he will be a good person for the job?

In your journal, respond to these questions:

The reporter said that the job of pronouncer [...] general public. Why do you think this is? [...] person becomes a pronouncer for the Nat[...] you like to train for the position?

After You Write   Edit

In the next chapter, you will learn abou[...] ment, you will not follow a formal revisio[...]

Comprehensive writing activities build students' understanding of the chapter topic and increase their academic writing skills.

CNN® video clips provide an exciting springboard for writing activities and help integrate listening skills.

6. Mothers in television are generally depicted as homebodies who aren't very intelligent.
7. Even the best father makes a mediocre mother.
8. I love my father very much.

ACADEMIC POWER STRATEGY

Apply the Strategy

Manage a large amount of information by making a chart that summarizes the information. This will also keep the information handy for future reference.

With some of your classmates, create an organizational checklist that lists the important qualities of paragraph structure, thesis statements, introductions, and conclusions using the format below. Then use this chart in the future to help you evaluate your essays for yourself.

ORGANIZATIONAL CHECKLIST

	Do this!	Don't do this!
Unity		
Topic Sentences		
Thesis Statements		
Introductions		
Conclusions		

Grammar You Can Use: "Perfect" Verbs and Time Frames

In Chapter 1 you learned that English writing shows a tendency to maintain time frames within paragraphs or portions of an essay. As you write your essay for this chapter, you will probably find it necessary to *briefly step out of a time frame.* That is, you may need to show differences in time while maintaining the overall time frame of a paragraph or portion of your essay. This is the main use for the "perfect verbs," which act as *bridges* between two times in English.

1. **Present perfect verbs** are present-tense verbs. They are often used to maintain a present time frame while referring to past events or to discuss events that began in the past but continue now.

Academic Power Strategies give students the knowledge and skills to become successful, independent learners.

Apply the Strategy activities encourage students to take charge of their learning and immediately use their new skills and strategies.

Integrated grammar instruction stems from the writing and reading activities, and gives students the know-how to write and edit their work with accuracy.

Tapestry Threads provide students with interesting facts and quotes that jumpstart classroom discussions.

Stimulating reading selections model writing and grammar usage, and prepare students for the pre-writing, writing, and revising activities.

Language Learning Strategies help students maximize their learning and become proficient in English.

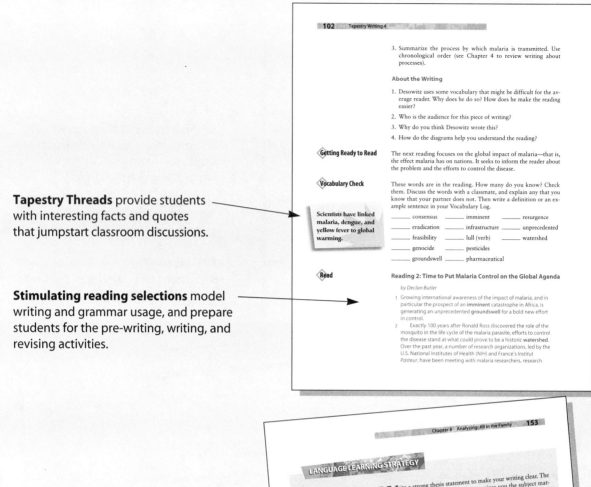

Test-Taking Tips offer students practical steps for improving their test results.

Check Your Progress helps students monitor their own progress.

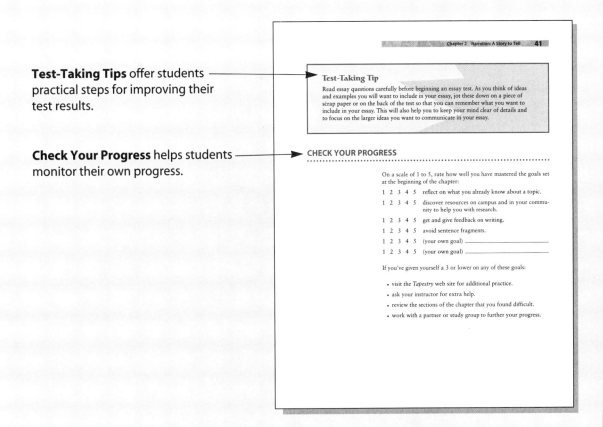

Test-Taking Tip

Read essay questions carefully before beginning an essay test. As you think of ideas and examples you will want to include in your essay, jot these down on a piece of scrap paper or on the back of the test so that you can remember what you want to include in your essay. This will also help you to keep your mind clear of details and to focus on the larger ideas you want to communicate in your essay.

CHECK YOUR PROGRESS

On a scale of 1 to 5, rate how well you have mastered the goals set at the beginning of the chapter:

1 2 3 4 5   reflect on what you already know about a topic.

1 2 3 4 5   discover resources on campus and in your community to help you with research.

1 2 3 4 5   get and give feedback on writing.

1 2 3 4 5   avoid sentence fragments.

1 2 3 4 5   (your own goal) _____

1 2 3 4 5   (your own goal) _____

If you've given yourself a 3 or lower on any of these goals:

- visit the *Tapestry* web site for additional practice.
- ask your instructor for extra help.
- review the sections of the chapter that you found difficult.
- work with a partner or study group to further your progress.

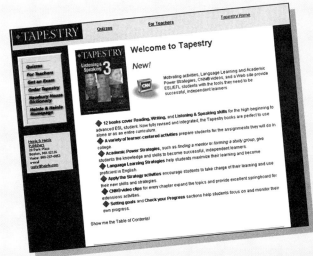

Expand your classroom at Tapestry Online
www.tapestry.heinle.com
- Online Quizzes
- Instructor's Manuals
- Opportunities to use and expand the Academic Power Strategies
- More!

For a well-integrated curriculum, try the **Tapestry Reading** series and the **Tapestry Listening & Speaking** series, also from Heinle & Heinle.

To learn more about the **Tapestry** principles, read *The Tapestry of Language Learning,* Second Edition, by Rebecca L. Oxford and Robin C. Scarcella, also from Heinle & Heinle Publishers. ISBN 0-8384-0994-6.

If you want to be successful in life, follow your heart and do what you love.

—paraphrased from
Marian Diamond

Do you agree with this quotation?

What do you think it means to be successful?

Who do you think is successful? Why?

STORIES OF SUCCESS

1

Success means different things to different people. Some people believe success is a good grade in school or an important position at work. Others believe success is a lot of money or fame. Still others think success is personal. They believe success is a happy life or good relationships with friends and family members. In this chapter you will read and write about different kinds of success. You will think about what you must be or do to be successful.

Setting Goals

In this chapter you will learn how to:

◈ write about someone who is successful.

In order to do this, you will:

◈ use freewriting to help you write what you already know and think of new ideas.

◈ use graphic organizers to organize your ideas.

◈ create a Writer's Portfolio to keep track of your learning.

◈ read some stories of success by and about immigrants.

◈ learn present- and past-tense verb forms.

**Getting Started**

What is success? How do you succeed? First, think about different kinds of success. Choose from these ideas and add one of your own. Then write them in the chart below under Column 1.

Kinds of Success

- a good job
- fame
- a lot of money
- freedom
- power
- an important professional position

Next, think about ways to achieve success. Write them in Column 2. Match the ideas in Column 1 and Column 2.

Ways to Achieve Success

- work hard
- get help
- be lucky
- have a dream
- be determined
- study

When you are finished, discuss your chart with a classmate. You and your classmate may have different charts.

Column 1: Kinds of Success	Column 2: Ways to Achieve Success
a good job	*study*

MEETING THE TOPIC

Talk with a Partner

Look at these people. Are they successful? Add two people you know to the list. Rate their success.

a.

	Not Successful ◄──► Very Successful				
a. Michael Jackson	1	2	3	4	5
b. Bill Clinton	1	2	3	4	5
c. Tiger Woods	1	2	3	4	5
d. Oprah Winfrey	1	2	3	4	5
e. Mahatma Gandhi	1	2	3	4	5
f. Bill Gates	1	2	3	4	5
g. Dalai Lama	1	2	3	4	5
h. Mother Teresa	1	2	3	4	5
i. _____	1	2	3	4	5
j. _____	1	2	3	4	5

Discuss your ratings with a partner. Explain why you think each person is (or isn't) successful.

b.

c.

d.

e.

f.

g.

h.

> Success is the accomplishment of a task, the reaching of a goal; a good event, wealth, good luck in life.
>
> —NEWBURY HOUSE DICTIONARY

◇ Freewrite

LANGUAGE LEARNING STRATEGY

Use freewriting to help you write what you already know and to think of new ideas. Freewriting is a good way to begin writing about a topic. When you freewrite, you write down all your ideas about a topic. You can write words, phrases, or sentences. Write quickly. Don't worry about spelling or grammar. Here is an example of one student's freewrite:

I don't write too much so this freewriting is very unusual. I don't have anything to say. To tell the truth, I didn't want to say even this. Maybe I don't write much because I'm not good at English. I think I should write more. This freewriting is not a bad idea.

—Hiroyuki Matsumaru

Apply the Strategy

Freewrite about a successful person you know. (You can write about yourself.) Answer any of these questions to begin. Then write some other things you know about this person.

- What does this person do?
- Where does this person come from?
- Why do you think this person is successful?
- How did this person become successful?

Write for at least ten minutes. You will use this writing later.

TUNING IN: "Kan's Dream for Success"

© CNN

The video you will watch is about a group of Vietnamese immigrants in the United States who have a dream for success. First, read the questions to focus your listening. Then watch the video and answer the questions.

1. What is the dream of these Vietnamese immigrants?

    a. to become teachers

    b. to become priests

    c. to return to their country

2. Which sentence is true?

    a. The priesthood has always been popular among immigrants.

    b. The priesthood has never been popular among immigrants.

3. Which sentence is not true?

    a. Kan Tran and his father tried to escape Vietnam eight times.

    b. Kan Tran's father does not want his son to become a priest.

    c. Kan Tran did not have religious freedom in his country.

4. What does Kan's father want for his son?

    a. whatever makes him famous

    b. whatever makes him happy

    c. whatever makes him rich

5. What is difficult for these men who want to become priests?

    a. English

    b. Vietnamese

    c. Spanish

6. What does Kan say?

    a. "I am pursuing success."

    b. "I am pursuing my dream."

    c. "I am pursuing my father's dream."

Wealth consists not in having outer possessions, but in having inner treasures.

—SUFI WISDOM

ACADEMIC POWER STRATEGY

Use a Writer's Portfolio to keep track of your learning. Collect the important work for this class in a folder, notebook, or binder. This is called a Writer's Portfolio. Your portfolio will help you keep all your work in one place and review your progress. Your teacher, one or more classmates, and maybe a friend will read your Writer's Portfolio during this course.

Apply the Strategy

Create your Writer's Portfolio. Choose a folder, notebook, or binder. Write *Writer's Portfolio* and your name on the front of the portfolio. Make at least three sections in the portfolio: one section for vocabulary, one section for freewriting, and one section for writing assignments. You may want to add a section for grammar and a section for new ideas. (In Chapter 7 you will create an Idea File.)

On the first page of your Writer's Portfolio, write a short letter to the person who will read your portfolio (your teacher, a classmate, a friend, yourself).

Dear Reader,

This is my Writer's Portfolio for (course title) _____,

(semester or beginning and end dates of course) _____.

My teacher's name is _____. I want to tell you about

my writing now. Here is what I do well when I write: I (one thing

you do well) _____, and I (another thing you do well)

_____. Here is what I want to improve when I write:

(one thing you don't do well) _____.

I want to add that (say one more thing about your writing)

_____

_____.

Sincerely,

(Your name) _____

EXPANDING YOUR LANGUAGE

◇ Vocabulary Check

In each chapter of this book, you will study vocabulary to help you with the writing assignment. The words and expressions come from the exercises and reading selections. Learn the definitions of new words and record them in the Vocabulary Section of your Writer's Portfolio. You should read the Vocabulary Section often to review the new words.

In this chapter, the words and expressions are about people and success. Check those that you know.

_____ achieve success		_____ lucky
_____ determined		_____ power
_____ earn a degree		_____ succeed
_____ fame		_____ success
_____ get a license		_____ successful
_____ give up		_____ unafraid
_____ hard-working		_____ vision
_____ have a dream		_____ win an award

◇ Vocabulary Building

1. Match the words from the Vocabulary Check to words on the right with the **opposite** meaning. These are **antonyms**.

achieve success	lazy
hard-working	unlucky
immigrant	continue
unafraid	fail
lucky	native
give up	afraid

2. Use the correct word or phrase to complete the following paragraph. This is from a book on college success.

successful	achieve success
give up	vision
determined	hard-working
power	success
have a dream	earn a degree

Be a Successful Student

(a) _____ is a choice. It can be your choice. Students who are (b) _____ to do well in school often (c) _____. Here are some tips for becoming a successful student. First, do you (d) _____ for the future? It is a good idea to have a (e) _____. Think about what you want to do. Then make a plan. It is not easy to be (f) _____ in a new culture using a new language. But it is possible if you are (g) _____. When you are tired or discouraged, don't (h) _____. You alone have the (i) _____ to choose success. That choice will help you (j) _____.

Grammar You Can Use: Past and Present Verb Tenses

The verb system in English is difficult to learn. Get an early start on using verbs correctly. Paying attention to verb tense will improve your writing.

Verbs are words that express action or existence. Verbs have:

- a **number** (singular or plural)
- a **point of view** (first person [*I* or *we*], second person [*you*], or third person [*he, she, it, they*])
- different **tenses** (present, past, future)

Use the **present tense** to write about something that is happening *now* or *regularly*. Use the **past tense** to write about something that happened *in the past*. When you write about a successful person, you can begin by *writing about the past* and then showing how a person is successful *in the present*. Look at the example:

*Sekuru **had** no work last year. Now he **is** a store clerk during the week and a waiter at a restaurant on the weekends.*

Review these verbs in present and past tense.

Verb	Present Tense	Past Tense
to be	I **am,** you/we/they **are,** he/she/it **is**	I/he/she/it **was,** you/we/they **were**
to do	I/you/we/they **do,** he/she/it **does**	I/you/we/they/he/she/it **did**
to have	I/you/we/they **have,** he/she/it **has**	I/you/we/they/he/she/it **had**

Verb	Present Tense	Past Tense
to study	I/you/we/they **study,** he/she/it **studies**	I/you/we/they/he/she/it **studied**
to get	I/you/we/they **get,** he/she/it **gets**	I/you/we/they/he/she/it **got**
to try	I/you/we/they **try,** he/she/it **tries**	I/you/we/they/he/she/it **tried**
to win	I/you/we/they **win,** he/she/it **wins**	I/you/we/they/he/she/it **won**

Practice using present- and past-tense verbs. First, go back to your freewrite and check your verb tenses. Correct any mistakes. Then answer these questions:

1. Write about a time in the past when you were successful. What did you do? Where were you? Did you get an award for your success?

   _____

   _____

   _____

2. Write about what you are studying now. What is your goal? What do you want to do after you finish your education?

   _____

   _____

   _____

LANGUAGE LEARNING STRATEGY

Use graphic organizers to write and organize your ideas. A **graphic organizer** is a "picture" of ideas. Writers use graphic organizers for thinking about and organizing ideas. There are many kinds of graphic organizers. Charts, graphs, diagrams, and outlines are examples of graphic organizers. You can use graphic organizers to understand the relationships among ideas.

(continued on next page)

One kind of graphic organizer is a **cluster**. Use a cluster to write information around a central idea. Here's an example of a cluster:

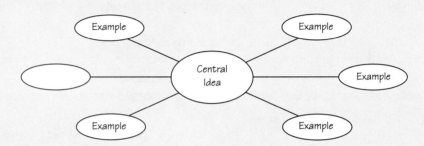

Apply the Strategy

Practice using graphic organizers. First make a cluster of your class. In the center of the cluster, write the name of the class and the name of the teacher. Then write the names of the students around the central idea. This will help you learn the names of your classmates.

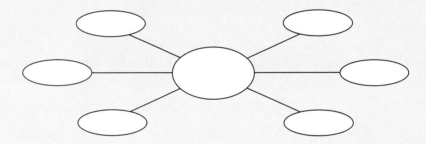

Now make a cluster about success. Write the word *success* in the center of the cluster. Then write around the central idea all of the ways you think a person can be successful. Begin by thinking about these ideas and adding some of your own:

fame	power	a lot of friends
a lot of money	an important position	good health

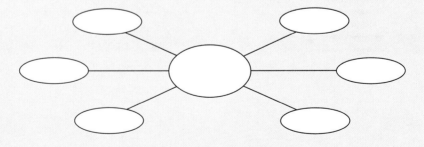

READING FOR WRITING

The stories of success you will read in this section come from newspaper articles. You will find words and ideas that will help you with the writing assignment in this chapter.

Reading 1 is about a man from Vietnam. Before you read, talk to a classmate and answer these questions:

- What is something a person can do to be helpful in his or her community?

- Some immigrants lose their native language and culture when they move to a new country. What is something immigrants can do to keep their language and culture strong?

Reading 1: A Modern American Success Story

Man Phan came from Vietnam. He had a difficult time when he first came to America. He didn't speak English, and he didn't have work. Now Phan does many things to help people. He lives in a community with people from many cultures. Phan teaches Vietnamese language and culture to Vietnamese children. He is a member of the Vietnamese-American Friendship group. He teaches Americans about Vietnamese customs too. Every morning Phan and his wife take a walk. They pick up bottles and cans. They want to keep their community clean. They get money for the bottles and cans and send it to orphans* in Vietnam. Phan **won an award** last week for outstanding service to his community. He is a modern American **success** story.

—Karen Nakamura

1. Reread "A Modern American Success Story." Underline the verbs in present tense. Put a circle around verbs in past tense.

2. Rewrite Phan's success story by using the sentences below and on the following page. Put them in the order they appear in the article.

   a. Phan won an award.

   b. Phan came from Vietnam.

   c. Phan recycles bottles and cans.

*orphans: children without parents

    d. Phan teaches Vietnamese language and culture.

    e. Phan had a difficult life when he first came to America.

    f. Phan helps people in his community.

3. Phan won some money as part of his award. What do you think Phan did with the money he won? Why?

_____

_____

_____

4. *Challenge Question:* Why is Phan's story a "modern success story"?

_____

_____

_____

Reading 2 is about a hard-working man from Japan. Before you read, talk to a classmate and answer these questions:

- Think of one hard-working person you know. What does this person do?

- Many immigrants come to the United States and Canada. What is one problem they have when they first arrive?

Reading 2: Unafraid of the Dark

1 When Toshiro Yamamoto was a boy in Japan, a soccer ball hit him in the face. He became blind[1] in one eye. When he was older, he became **successful** in massage[2] and acupuncture.[3] Later he came to the United States with his family. He wanted to continue his work, but he needed a license in his new country.

2   Now Toshiro is studying at City College of San Francisco. However, because of an unusual condition, he is losing sight in his other eye. Soon he will transfer to San Francisco State University. He wants to **earn a degree** and **get a license**. Toshiro is **determined** and **hard-working**. He is losing his eyesight, but not his **vision** to be successful.

—Joe Brown

[1]**blind:** unable to see

[2]**massage:** rubbing the muscles for relaxation and pain relief

[3]**acupuncture:** Chinese medical treatment that relieves pain by putting needles into the body

> **Success is patience and persistence.**
>
> **—SARAH BAN BREATHNACH**

1. Put the sentences in the right order. Then rewrite Toshiro's success story, using as many of your own words as you can.

   a. Toshiro came to the United States.

   b. Toshiro was hit by a ball.

   c. Toshiro worked in Japan.

   d. Toshiro lost sight in one eye.

   e. Toshiro studied in the United States.

   f. Toshiro began to lose sight in his other eye.

2. Are these sentences true or false? Rewrite the false sentences. Make them true.

   a. _____ Toshiro lives in Japan today.

   _____

   b. _____ Toshiro doesn't work hard.

   _____

   c. _____ Toshiro can see perfectly.

   _____

3. *Challenge Question:* What do you think the title "Unafraid of the Dark" means?

   a. Toshiro is not afraid of becoming blind.

   b. Toshiro is not afraid to work hard to become successful.

   c. Both of these.

FROM READING TO WRITING

▷ **Getting Ready to Write**

Choose a Topic

In this chapter, you are going to write about a successful person. Choose a person who is successful in one of these ways:

- The person is an excellent student.
- The person is hard-working.
- The person is successful in his or her career.
- The person has a lot of money.
- The person graduated from college. ⚹
- The person is famous.
- The person is happy.
- The person lives life in his or her own way.

Choose your topic and write it here:

I will write about _____

_____

_____

_____ .

Here are some instructions for writing:

Instructions for Writing About a Successful Person

1. In this chapter, you have read about success stories that describe **the past**. It is easier to show how a person is successful by comparing the past and the present. For your writing assignment, **begin with the past**. Here are some examples from this chapter:

- *Two years ago my English was so bad.*
- *Man Phan came from Vietnam.*
- *When Toshiro Yamamoto was a boy in Japan, a soccer ball hit him in the face.*

2. You have talked, read, and written about different kinds of success in this chapter. You've seen that people can be successful in many ways. When you write, **explain what kind of success** your person shows. Here are some examples from this chapter:

   - *Now Phan does many things to help people.*
   - *He wants to earn a degree and get a license.*
   - *Now my English is better.*

3. You have also thought about several ways people become successful. When you write, describe **how the person achieved success.** This is the most interesting part of your writing. Here are some examples from this chapter:

   - *I studied every weekend and on holidays.*
   - *Toshiro is determined and hard-working.*
   - *Every day after school I studied hard to learn more.*

Study a Student Example

It is useful to read how other students have written about the same topic. Before you write, read this story of success by a community college student. He writes about himself.

Two Years and Many Changes

Two years ago my English was so bad. I didn't understand and I couldn't speak. Every day after school I studied hard to learn more. I didn't help my sisters with their homework. I didn't like to go to the library. I studied every weekend and on holidays. Now my English is better. Now I try my best to help my sisters when they have problems. I like to go to the library to borrow books. One thing that hasn't changed is that I still study hard.

—Tharavouth Tan

1. Write two things that changed for Tharavouth. Complete the Before and After chart.

Before	After
He didn't like to go to the library.	*He likes to go to the library.*

2. Why do you think Tharavouth was successful?

_____

_____

_____

_____

_____

3. What is one thing you noticed and liked about Tharavouth's writing?

_____

_____

_____

_____

4. What is one question or suggestion you have?

_____

_____

_____

_____

_____

 Write

Now write a story of success using the topic you chose in Getting Ready to Write. Follow the instructions. You may use the writing you began in the Freewrite activity and any of the exercises from this chapter.

After You Write

When you **revise**, you look at the development of ideas. When you **edit**, you look for organization and language. You will revise and edit what you write in every chapter in order to improve your writing.

Revise

First, read these questions and review your own writing. Then have someone else look at your writing. Your classmate will complete these statements:

1. The writing is about **this successful person:**

   _____

   _____

2. This person shows **this kind of success:**

   _____

   _____

3. This person **achieved success in this way:**

   _____

   _____

4. I have this question or suggestion for the writer:

   _____

   _____

   _____

Make changes to improve the development of ideas in your writing.

Edit

Now have someone check your writing for organization and language. Give your revised writing to a classmate. Your classmate will answer these questions:

1. Does the writer use **present and past verb tenses** correctly? Yes   No

   If the answer is no, which verbs should be corrected?

   _____

   _____

2. Does the writer use **words and expressions from this chapter** correctly?   Yes   No

   If the answer is no, which words should be corrected?

   _____

   _____

3. Are there any other **language mistakes**?   Yes   No

   If the answer is yes, write one or two of them here.

   _____

   _____

Make corrections to your organization and language. Now, after final revisions, your teacher will ask you to hand in your writing for a grade or put it in your Writer's Portfolio. You will review your writing assignment later.

PUTTING IT ALL TOGETHER

◆ **Use What You Have Learned**

1. Write about another person who is successful. This person can be someone famous or someone you know. Try to write more quickly this time and use what you learned in this chapter.

2. Write your own story of success. Write about yourself now or in the future. How did you achieve success? How will you achieve success?

3. Write a fan letter to a successful person you admire. In your letter, explain how you know about this person and why you admire him or her. Before you send the letter, read it to your classmates.

Test-Taking Tip

Learn as much as you can about essay tests in order to prepare for them effectively. Ask your teacher if you will be able to use books or notes. Ask if there will be one long question, or if there will be a few shorter questions. Try to predict what the essay questions will be, based on the work you have done in class.

CHECK YOUR PROGRESS

On a scale of 1 to 5, where 1 means "not at all," 2 means "not very well," 3 means "moderately well," 4 means "well," and 5 means "very well," rate how well you have mastered the goals set at the beginning of the chapter:

1 2 3 4 5   write about someone who is successful.

1 2 3 4 5   use freewriting to help you write what you already know and think of new ideas.

1 2 3 4 5   use graphic organizers to organize your ideas.

1 2 3 4 5   create a Writer's Portfolio to keep track of your learning.

1 2 3 4 5   learn present- and past-tense verb forms.

If you've given yourself a 3 or lower on any of these goals:

- visit the *Tapestry* web site for additional practice.

- ask your instructor for extra help.

- review the sections of the chapter that you found difficult.

- work with a partner or study group to further your progress.

"You are a product of your environment. So choose the environment that will best develop you toward your objective."

—W. Clement Stone

How does the space in the photo make you feel?

Do certain colors or smells affect your feelings?

Do you agree with the quotation?

2

SPACES THAT WORK

Do you have certain feelings in different spaces? Most people do, although we don't always pay attention to those feelings. In this chapter you will read and write about spaces. You'll read about how spaces affect our feelings and our actions. After reading and thinking, you will write about a space that helps you work well.

Setting Goals

In this chapter you will learn how to:

◈ write about a space that affects what you do and how you feel.

In order to do this, you will:

◈ learn to use new words and expressions as soon as you can to remember them and use them correctly.

◈ learn to work in drafts to improve your writing.

◈ set goals in order to focus your learning.

◈ read two selections about spaces that work.

◈ learn how to use countable and noncountable nouns in your writing.

ACADEMIC POWER STRATEGY

*S*et goals in order to focus your learning. When people know what they want to achieve, they can reach their goal faster. This is especially true for students. When students set learning goals, they can focus their energy and save time. Here are some examples of learning goals:

- *I want to find a place to study where I can think clearly and do good work.*
- *My goal is to learn to write about many different topics.*
- *I will keep all my writing and review it to see my progress.*
- *I will prepare for college courses.*

Apply the Strategy

In each chapter of this book, you set goals and you check your progress. Think about one important goal you have for your writing in this course. You will check your progress on this goal at the end of the course. Write it below:

_____

_____

◇ Getting Started

Colors have a profound effect on your health and well-being. Blue makes you calm, and red makes you energetic.

Think about where you go every day. Think about places where you spend time. Are there places—rooms, buildings, areas—that affect how you feel? Are there places where you can work fast? Think clearly? Feel happy? Feel smart? Begin to think about this topic by completing a chart.

First, in Column 1, write the names of places where you spend your time. Then, in Column 2, write how these places affect you. Do they help you act or feel a certain way? First, read the example. Complete the chart, and when you finish, share your writing with a classmate.

Column 1: Places Where You Spend Time	Column 2: How These Places Affect You
Cafe 65 (a coffee shop)	I am in a hurry when I am here. There is a lot of noise. I do homework. I work fast.

Column 1: Places Where You Spend Time	Column 2: How These Places Affect You

MEETING THE TOPIC

Talk with a Partner

With a partner, look at the following photos. Would you want to spend time in these places? Why or why not? What would you do here? Write answers below each picture.

_____

_____

_____

_____

_____

_____

◆ **Freewrite**

Freewrite about a place that affects what you do and how you feel. Answer any of these questions to begin. Then write some other ideas about the place and your feelings.

- Where is this place?
- What do you see, hear, smell in this place?
- When do you go there?
- Why do you go there?
- How does this place make you feel?

Write quickly to record all of your ideas. You will use your freewrite again to prepare for the assignment.

TUNING IN: "Feng Shui Around the World"

© CNN

How do you decide where to put furniture in your room? One philosophy, originally from China, claims that there is invisible energy that affects our daily lives. This is called *Feng Shui*. This philosophy suggests ways to have positive energy around you. Watch the video and answer the questions. You will read about *Feng Shui* later in the chapter.

Homebuilders in northern California are learning about *Feng Shui* in order to sell homes to their many Asian customers.

1. *Feng Shui* is an ancient science of
    a. the flow of energy.
    b. Chinese history.
    c. music.

2. *Feng Shui* can affect
    a. relationships.
    b. business success.
    c. both of these.

3. Some people don't believe in *Feng Shui*. They think it is
    a. an external force.
    b. superstition.
    c. both of these.

4. *Feng Shui* can help people

   a. create a supportive environment.

   b. learn a new language.

   c. find a husband or wife.

5. Which sentence is true?

   a. People in many parts of the world practice *Feng Shui*.

   b. Only Chinese people practice *Feng Shui*.

   c. Very few Chinese people practice *Feng Shui*.

6. Where was this video filmed?

   a. China

   b. the United States

   c. the Philippines

EXPANDING YOUR LANGUAGE

◇ Vocabulary Check

The following words and expressions will help you with the reading and writing in this chapter. Check those that you know. Work with a partner to learn the definitions of new words and add them to the Vocabulary Section of your Writer's Portfolio.

_____ affect

_____ balance

_____ confident

_____ environment

_____ flow of energy

_____ harmony

_____ have an effect on

_____ heal

_____ make someone feel (happy, sad, etc.)

_____ pain

_____ place

_____ pleasant-looking

_____ practice (a profession)

_____ space

_____ take one's mind off one's problems

◈ Vocabulary Building

1. Each word in Column 1 is from the Vocabulary Check. Circle the word in Column 2 with the same meaning.

COLUMN 1	COLUMN 2			
heal	place	get well	design
environment	minds	pain	surroundings
confident	ancient	strong	energetic
affect	influence	practice	write
harmony	minds	therapy	balance
space	universe	area	planet
pain	money	window	injury

2. Complete the following paragraph by using these words:

   place

   space

   environment

   peaceful

A Traditional Chinese Home

A traditional Chinese home is a _____ of private beauty. It has walls around it. There is a courtyard in the center and a pleasant-looking garden. There is no view. The only open _____ is the sky above. A Chinese person is happy to spend time at home. It is a calm _____ where he or she can relax and be _____ .

3. Use this paragraph frame to write a paragraph about where you live.

My home is _____ . It has _____ around it. There is a _____ and a _____ . There is no _____ . My home is a place where I can _____ and be _____ .

LANGUAGE LEARNING STRATEGY

Apply the Strategy

Use new words as soon as you can. You will remember the meanings of new words if you use them immediately. You will also learn how to write new words correctly if you use them right away. Use new words when you talk and especially when you write. You will increase your English vocabulary quickly this way.

Here are some ways people feel in certain places:

calm	relaxed	nervous
happy	stressed	confident
energetic		

Use these words in your own sentences. Write about how *you* feel in three of these public places:

in airports	in the classroom	at the hospital
at the supermarket	in coffee shops	at the post office
at the library		

(continued on next page)

I always feel nervous in airports. They are crowded, and everyone is always in a hurry.

_____

_____

_____

_____

_____

_____

Grammar You Can Use: Countable and Noncountable Nouns

A **noun** is a word that is the name of a person, place, thing, or idea. Nouns can be countable or noncountable.

Countable nouns need *a, an,* or *the* before them. Here are some countable nouns from this chapter:

a place, the environment, an effect

Noncountable nouns need *the, some,* or nothing before them. They take the third-person singular verb form. Here are some noncountable nouns from this chapter:

harmony, energy

When you write about spaces, you will use countable and noncountable nouns. Practice using them correctly by completing the following paragraph. Choose countable (C) and noncountable (NC) words from the lists below. Read your paragraph to a classmate when you are finished. Your answers may be different.

COUNTABLE	NONCOUNTABLE
table	hot chocolate
coffee shop	energy
place	bread
class	work
college	coffee
window	hair
person	
smile	
cafe	

Cafe 65

Cafe 65 is a well-known (C) _____ among students because it's next to the (C) _____. In the morning, it's very crowded. Students drink (NC) _____ and talk and get ready for their first (C) _____. There is lots of (NC) _____ and noise. In the afternoon, the (C)_____ is quiet. There is one (C) _____ who works at Cafe 65. She is very friendly. She has brown (NC) _____ and a big (C) _____. When I go to Cafe 65, I sit at a (C) _____ near the (C) _____. I usually drink (NC) _____, and I eat some (NC) _____. Students do a lot of (NC) _____ at Cafe 65. It is a good (C) _____ for busy students.

READING FOR WRITING

You will read about two environments that have an effect on how people act and feel. These readings will help you with your writing in this chapter.

Reading 1 is from a news article about a space that helps hospital patients get well. Before you read, talk to a classmate and answer these questions:

• When you are sick, what sights, sounds, and smells help you feel better?

• Plan a room for sick people. What do the people see? Hear? Smell?

Reading 1: Mitch Leichter's Magical Recreation Room

> Sounds of nature, such as ocean waves and rainfall, bring feelings of peace and relaxation.

Everything in Mitch Leichter's magical recreation room is just perfect. Perfect, that is, for his hospital patients. There are beautiful fish swimming in aquariums, pools of gentle waterfalls, soft classical music, and smells of flower gardens, apple pies, and pine trees in the forest. There are puppies and kittens for patients to hold and books and magazines to read. "People want to forget their **pain**," Leichter says. So he designed an **environment** where patients can "**take their minds off**" their problems. "It's amazing," he exclaims. "People feel better and **heal** faster. Smells, music, and pets **have a powerful effect on** the minds and bodies of these patients."

—Dennis McCarthy

1. What are two things in Mitch Leichter's magical recreation room?

    a. _____

    b. _____

2. How do patients feel in Mitch Leichter's magical recreation room?

   a. pleasant-looking

   b. better

   c. forgetful

3. Add something to Mitch Leichter's magical recreation room. Explain how it helps people feel better.

   _____

   _____

   _____

   _____

   _____

   _____

   _____

4. *Challenge Question:* Mitch's idea is called *environmental therapy.* Do people in your native culture practice environmental therapy?

   _____

   _____

   _____

   _____

   _____

   _____

   _____

   Reading 2 is a news article about the ancient Chinese science of placing objects in a room. *Feng Shui* was the subject of the video in this chapter. Before you read, answer these questions:

   • Had you heard of *Feng Shui* before reading this chapter? Where? How?

   • Do you think that the place where you live has a "positive energy flow"? How do you know?

Reading 2: Bring Positive Energy into Your Home

Feng Shui is an ancient Chinese art. It teaches how to place objects in a room. The expression means "wind" and "water." *Feng Shui* tries to **balance** *chi*, energy from the universe and energy from the earth. People who **practice** *Feng Shui* place light (lamps), sounds (bells), and living objects (plants and fish) carefully in their homes and businesses to create a **flow of energy.** They believe that *chi* can bring them success with their careers, children, relationships, and health. There are many stories of success from people who **practice** *Feng Shui.* Janet Angier's story is an example. She began to **practice** *Feng Shui* by hanging round glass balls from the ceiling. She put a mirror by her front door and turned her desk away from the window. A short time later she received $55,000 from extra taxes she had paid and the settlement of a court case. Her business started to grow, and she felt more **confident.** She says it's all because of *Feng Shui.* This method of achieving **harmony** is becoming well-known and quite popular for people like Janet. Companies are also bringing in *Feng Shui* to improve their business.

—Olivia Barker

> U.S. companies, like Esprit de Corps, are using *Feng Shui* to improve the work environment and increase profits.
>
> —*SAN FRANCISCO CHRONICLE*

1. *Feng Shui* is:

   a. a place in China.

   b. the art of balancing energy in a space.

   c. the study of the universe and the earth.

2. What are some things that a person practicing *Feng Shui* does?

   a. moves a bed to face the window

   b. places a plant near a door

   c. both of these

3. Write at least three sentences about how objects, light, color, or noise affect how you feel.

   _____

   _____

   _____

4. What do you think about *Feng Shui*? Do you believe that the balance of energy in one's home or office can affect one's success? Write your opinion below.

   I believe that *Feng Shui* _____

   _____

FROM READING TO WRITING

◆Getting Ready to Write

Choose a Topic

You have read about how environments affect how we feel and what we are able to do. Now you are going to write about a place that affects you. Choose one of these ways:

- The place makes you work hard.
- The place makes you feel relaxed, calm, and peaceful.
- The place makes you feel energetic.
- The place makes you feel sad, uncomfortable, and terrible.
- The place always makes you think about the same thing.

Write your topic here:

I will write about _____

_____

Follow these instructions when you write:

Instructions for Writing About Spaces That Work

1. **Describe** the space. Help your reader "see" the environment. Following are some examples of description in this chapter:

- *There are beautiful fish swimming in aquariums, pools of gentle waterfalls, soft classical music, and smells of flower gardens, apple pies, and pine trees in the forest.*

- *The room is organized and pleasant-looking. It has a thick brown carpet on the floor and a large window.*

2. Explain **what you do** or **how you feel** in this space. Look at these examples:

- *People feel better and heal faster.*

- *Chi can bring success with careers, children, relationships, and health.*

- *I can relax and concentrate when I go to my study.*

3. Explain **why** the space **helps you do something** or **feel a certain way.** Read these examples:

- *Smells, music, and pets have a powerful effect on the minds and bodies of these patients.*

- *Feng Shui tries to balance chi, energy from the universe and energy from the earth.*

- *Because of the sights and smells, I can relax and concentrate.*

Study a Student Example

Before you write, read this paragraph by a community college student.

My Study

My study is a big room on the second floor of my house. The room is organized and **pleasant-looking.** It has a thick brown carpet on the floor and a large window. I can look through the window and see a magnificent green lawn, some lovely roses and a few fruit trees. There is a golden apple tree, a pear tree and my favorite: a

Fuji persimmon tree. If I sit in my study with the window open, I can smell roses in the summer and I can smell orange blossoms from orchards about a half-mile away around Christmas. After dinner I usually read or write or study. Because of the sights and smells, I can relax and concentrate when I go to my study.

—Tharavouth Tan

1. What can Tharavouth **not** do in his study?

   a. relax

   b. cook

   c. study

2. What does Tharavouth write about in "My Study"?

   a. what he sees   d. what he does

   b. what he smells   e. all of these

   c. how he feels

   d. what he does

3. What is one thing you noticed and liked about Tharavouth's writing?

   _____

4. What is one question or suggestion you have?

   _____

◆**Write**

Now write about a space that affects you, using the topic you chose on page 35. Review what you've learned in this chapter and the writing you've already done.

◆**After You Write**

LANGUAGE LEARNING STRATEGY

Work in drafts to improve your writing. All writers—student writers and professional writers—write their pieces several times. Each time they write, it is called a **draft**. In each draft, the writing gets better. Some students are surprised to learn that writers rewrite pieces

(continued on next page)

three or more times before they complete their **final draft**. Be prepared to write assignments at least two times. This way, you will make your ideas easier to understand, and you will correct language mistakes.

Apply the Strategy

Revise

First, have someone look at the **ideas** in your writing. Give your finished paragraph to a classmate. Your classmate will complete these statements:

1. The writing is about this space: _____

2. The writer describes the space so that I   can   cannot   "see" it.

3. This is what the writer does when in the space:

   _____

4. This is how the writer feels when in the space:

   _____

5. The writer could add or change this to improve the paragraph:

   _____

Make changes to improve the development of ideas in your writing.

Edit

Now have someone check your writing for **organization** and **language**. Give your revised paragraph to a classmate. Your classmate will answer these questions:

1. Does the writer begin with a description of the space?
   Yes   No

2. Does the writer use countable and uncountable nouns correctly?
   Yes   No

   If the answer is no, which words should be corrected?

   _____

3. Are there any language mistakes? (Please write them here.)
   Yes   No

   _____

Make corrections to your organization and language.

PUTTING IT ALL TOGETHER

◇ **Use What You Have Learned**

1. Write about another space. Choose a space that affects you in a different way. If you already wrote about a place where you study, write about a place where you have fun. Explain how the place makes you feel.

2. Watch the film *Patch Adams*. It is the story of a medical student who has some unusual ideas about hospital patients. How are Patch Adams and Mitch Leichter similar? Write or talk about three similarities.

Test-Taking Tip

After you have tried to predict the questions that will appear on a test, practice writing your answers to these questions. This will help you organize your thoughts and will also help you review vocabulary you want to include in the essay. Practicing your essay-writing before the test will help give you confidence on the day of the test.

CHECK YOUR PROGRESS

On a scale of 1 to 5, rate how well you have mastered the goals set at the beginning of the chapter:

1 2 3 4 5 write about a space that affects what you do and how you feel.

1 2 3 4 5 learn to use new words and expressions as soon as you can.

1 2 3 4 5 learn to work in drafts to improve your writing.

1 2 3 4 5 set goals in order to focus your learning.

1 2 3 4 5 learn how to use countable and noncountable nouns in your writing.

If you've given yourself a 3 or lower on any of these goals:

• visit the *Tapestry* web site for additional practice.

• ask your instructor for extra help.

• review the sections of the chapter that you found difficult.

• work with a partner or study group to further your progress.

"I don't believe in age."

—Pablo Neruda

Do the people in the photo look young or old?

What do you think Pablo Neruda means?

Describe a "typical" older person.

Describe a "typical" younger person.

3

NEVER TOO OLD

They say that the United States is "graying." That is, people are living longer and longer. What are these sixty-, seventy-, eighty-, and even ninety-year olds doing with their time? Some continue to work. Others travel. Still others begin new projects and learn new skills. They work and play hard. In this chapter you will read and think about active seniors; then you will write about a person you know.

Setting Goals

In this chapter you will learn how to:

◈ write a paragraph about an active senior you know.

In order to do this, you will:

◈ learn parts of speech to write more correct sentences.

◈ learn how to read actively in order to improve your writing.

◈ make an Active Learner Plan.

◈ read two selections about active seniors.

◈ practice using rules of capitalization in order to write correctly.

Getting Started

Think of two people you know who are over sixty. What do they do every day? Are they busy? Are they active? Write down what they do. Then talk about them to a classmate.

THINGS THEY DO EVERY DAY

PEOPLE OVER 60	Morning	Afternoon	Evening
Person 1			
Person 2			

MEETING THE TOPIC

Talk with a Partner

With a partner, look at the photos. Match the descriptions to the pictures.

California has more seniors than any other state in the United States. In 2020 there will be 5.36 million people age sixty-five or older.

a.

b.

c.

d.

e.

f.

1. _____ Dick Emory is eighty years old. He is a flower grower. He travels to tropical countries to study orchids.

2. _____ Wakesa is ninety years old. He is a Maasai elder. He settles disputes, gives advice, and tells stories.

3. _____ Jerri Rondoni is seventy-three years old. She is a pilot. She delivers food and supplies to poor communities.

4. _____ Harlan Begay is sixty years old. He heals ill people. He is a Navajo medicine man.

5. _____ Ma-ma is sixty-eight years old. She takes care of her grandsons.

6. _____ Frank Morton is seventy-five years old. He is a clockmaker in Canada. He builds and repairs broken clocks and watches.

Now ask and answer these questions.

- When does old age begin?
- Is it good to be old in your native culture?
- Do you know some old people who act young?
- Do you know some young people who act old?

Freewrite

Freewrite about an active person over the age of fifty whom you know or knew. If you can't think of anyone you know, write about a famous person. Answer any of these questions to begin. Then write some other things you know about this person.

- What is the person's name?
- How do you know this person?
- How old is the person?
- Where does the person live?
- What does the person do?

Write as much as you can. Try to write quickly. You will use this writing later as you develop language and ideas for the assignment.

Grammar You Can Use: Capital Letters

Use capital letters for

- the first word in every sentence:

  My grandmother is 86 years old. She speaks four languages.

- races, nationalities, languages, and religions:

  My grandmother speaks French, Polish, Hebrew, and English. She is Jewish American.

- names of people and places:

  *Every week my grandmother visits her friend **Janet** at **Gerstle Park.***

- words like *mother*, *father*, and *uncle* when they are titles:

  *Grandmother is also a great cook. **Master Chef Liu** learned to cook from **Grandmother.***

- days of the week and months of the year:

  *I eat at my grandmother's every night after school. I have classes **Monday** through **Friday**. In **December** I spend every weekend with my grandmother.*

1. Answer at least four of these questions. Pay attention to capital letters.

   a. What country are you from? List two different countries that other students in your class come from.

      _____

      _____

   b. What is your native language? List two different languages that other students in your class speak.

      _____

      _____

   c. When is your birthday? When do two other students celebrate their birthdays?

      _____

      _____

   d. What days do you have English class?

      _____

      _____

   e. What is your teacher's name?

      _____

   f. In what month did your English class begin? When will it end?

      _____

      _____

Bringing People Together is a dating service in Florida. It specializes in senior citizens. The service helps men who are into their nineties. It rejects women at age eighty.

2. Read the paragraph. Correct the words that need capital letters.

people today are leading active lives as they grow older. earl shaffer, 79, just finished hiking the appalachian trail. jim tatum bicycled across the u.s.a. american seniors are traveling to all parts of the world. kayo nimura, 64, has traveled to paris, egypt, and thailand. in january she will go to laos and vietnam.

TUNING IN: "Online Grandpa"

You'll watch a video about someone who has chosen to keep learning. He is dismayed, or sad, because so many people his age are smart, but they don't spend their time in useful ways. Read the questions and watch the video; then answer the questions. Watch the video several times to check your answers.

1. How old is Walter Weiss, and how does he spend his time?

    a. He's fifty, and he teaches a computer class.

    b. He's seventy-three, and he spends time at his computer.

    c. He's seventy-three, and he's a bartender.

2. How many web pages does Walter have?

    a. one

    b. two

    c. three

3. How do some other people Walter's age spend their time?

    a. playing golf

    b. watching daytime TV

    c. both of these

4. Walter increases his computer skills at a computer class through a large adult education program. How many seventy-year-olds have taken this class?

    a. a few

    b. several

    c. hundreds

© CNN

5. What does Walter's teacher **not** say about him?

    a. "Walter should retire."

    b. "Walter has chosen to keep learning."

    c. "Walter keeps pushing himself."

6. What does Walter believe computers help you do?

    a. meet other seniors

    b. be in touch with the future

    c. appreciate daytime TV

LANGUAGE LEARNING STRATEGY

Use active reading strategies to improve your **writing**. Good writers read a lot. They read to get ideas for their writing. They also read to look at models, or examples, of good writing. One way to read actively is to **make notes as you read**. Here are some things you can do to be an active reader:

- **Circle or star** important words or phrases. This will help you learn vocabulary and see how it is used in sentences.

- **Highlight or underline** important phrases or sentences with a colored marker, pen or pencil. This will help you remember important ideas in the reading. It will also show you ways of ordering your important ideas when you write.

- **Write your own words next to what you read.** This will help you understand and remember the meaning of the reading.

Use active reading strategies when you read another person's writing. Study how one student has used active reading strategies:

Seniors Are Living Longer

main idea—first sentence / increasing = going up, higher	The age of seniors is (increasing.)
sentence #2 explains first sentence	People are living longer. Men* and
*men/women/themselves = plural	women* who take care of themselves* *are*
to turn (an age) = to become (an age)	*turning 60, 70, and 80.* And they are
healthy = well, in good health	living (healthy) lives.

Apply the Strategy

Use active reading strategies as you read the end of the article:

> There are many ways seniors take care
> of themselves. First, they eat healthy food.
> Second, they get regular exercise. Finally,
> they have friends. These people are active
> and happy in their old age.

EXPANDING YOUR LANGUAGE

◇ **Vocabulary Check**

These words and expressions come from the reading selections in this chapter. They will help you prepare for the writing assignment. Check those that you know. Learn the definitions of words you don't know and add them to the Vocabulary Section of your Writer's Portfolio.

> **After age seventy-five,
> there are four single
> women for every
> single man.**

_____ active

_____ attitude

_____ be, turn, become, reach
(the age of)

_____ be determined

_____ believe in something

_____ exercise

_____ healthy

_____ live a (healthy, active,
unhealthy, long) life

_____ mental, mentally

_____ physical

_____ positive

_____ regular, regularly

_____ senior

_____ take care of yourself/
your health

◇ **Vocabulary Building**

1. Use these words and expressions in sentences about the photos in Meeting the Topic on page 42.

take care of their health   mentally active

physical exercise   positive attitude

   a. Frank stays _____. He has so many watches to repair.

   b. Harlan helps Native Americans _____.

   c. Dick gets _____ when he walks in the jungle to find rare flowers.

   d. Jerri's _____ helps people who are in difficult situations.

   Write two more sentences using the vocabulary from this chapter.

   e. _____

   f. _____

2. Write your own sentences from these word sets. Use the words in any order.

   a. healthy   regular   exercise

   Example: *My great-aunt stays **healthy** because she gets **regular exercise**.*

   _____

   b. age   positive   attitude

   _____

   c. active   exercise   healthy life

   _____

3. Answer these questions using words and expressions from the Vocabulary Check.

   a. What do **seniors** in your native country do to **take care of their health?**

   _____

   b. Think of a person you know who **is over fifty** and who doesn't **take care of his or her health**. What does this person do?

   _____

c. *Challenge Question:* Which is more important, **mental exercise** or **physical exercise**? Explain your answer.

_____

_____

4. You have learned new vocabulary from three chapters about three different topics. This is a good time to review the Vocabulary Section of your Writer's Portfolio. Study the words and expressions you still find difficult. How many new words and expressions have you learned?

      a. 10–20   b. 20–40   c. 40–60

LANGUAGE LEARNING STRATEGY

Learn the parts of speech and know how to use them. All words in English belong to a group. You will learn four of the groups in this chapter and four more groups in Chapter 5. These groups are called **parts of speech.** Words in the same group are used in the same way. Learning the parts of speech and how to use them will help you write correct sentences. Here are four parts of speech:

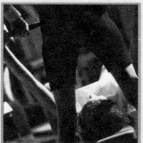

noun (a person, a place, a thing, or an idea)
    Uncle George, friend, exercise, tip
    *Jin's **aunt** rides a **bicycle** for **exercise.***

pronoun (a word used in place of a noun)
    I, she, you, it, their, us
    *Jin's aunt and uncle wanted to learn how to lift weights. **He** showed **them** how to do **it.***

verb (a word that expresses action or existence)
    is, exercise, does, played, understand
    *Jim Tatum **is** an active senior. He **turned** seventy-seven on December 11 last year.*

adjective (a word used to describe a noun or pronoun)
    active, busy, old, past, healthy
    *Leanne's **younger** sister is seventy-seven. She paints **beautiful** pictures.*

(continued on next page)

Apply the Strategy

1. Complete the following sentences. Use the part of speech indicated. Choose from these words.

Nouns	Pronouns	Verbs	Adjectives
race	He	is	older
morning	he	wakes up	good
		runs	His

Doc Sinclair (verb) ＿＿＿＿＿＿ an eighty-one-year-old athlete. (Pronoun) ＿＿＿＿＿＿ (verb) ＿＿＿＿＿＿ every (noun) ＿＿＿＿＿＿ at 4:00 A.M. He (verb) ＿＿＿＿＿＿ seven miles. At 6:00 A.M. (pronoun) ＿＿＿＿＿＿ swims. He doesn't swim fast. He says he's not very (adjective) ＿＿＿＿＿＿, but last year he won a (noun) ＿＿＿＿＿＿. He's just (adjective) ＿＿＿＿＿＿ than all the other athletes. (adjective) ＿＿＿＿＿＿ next competition is in two months. Good luck, Doc!

2. Use the paragraph frame to write about someone you know. Add the missing words. You can make the sentences longer (or shorter) or add sentences. Read your paragraph to the class when you are finished.

(Noun) ＿＿＿＿＿＿ (verb) ＿＿＿＿＿＿ a/an (adjective) ＿＿＿＿＿＿ (noun) ＿＿＿＿＿＿. (Pronoun) ＿＿＿＿＿＿ (verb) ＿＿＿＿＿＿ every (noun) ＿＿＿＿＿＿. (Pronoun) ＿＿＿＿＿＿ also (verb) ＿＿＿＿＿＿. (Noun) ＿＿＿＿＿＿ doesn't (verb) ＿＿＿＿＿＿. (Pronoun) ＿＿＿＿＿＿ says (pronoun) ＿＿＿＿＿＿ (verb) ＿＿＿＿＿＿. I think (noun) ＿＿＿＿＿＿ (verb) ＿＿＿＿＿＿ (adjective) ＿＿＿＿＿＿.

Sometimes one word can be several parts of speech. For example, look at how *senior* can be both a noun and an adjective:

I know three **seniors** who swim at the gym every day. (noun)

My grandmother is a **senior** citizen, so she rides the bus free. (adjective)

Read the following sentences and answer the questions.

3. Is **age** used as a verb or noun in these sentences?

    a. He looks young. I can't tell his **age.** _____

    b. She **is aging** so well. She is very healthy. _____

4. Is **exercise** used as a verb, a noun, or an adjective?

    a. Peter **exercises** with his son. They use machines at the gym. _____

    b. Marthe takes an **exercise** class after work. _____

    c. Juan gets lots of **exercise** at his job. _____

READING FOR WRITING

Felix and Clara Kirschling have birthdays three days apart. This year they turned 100. They were married 47 years ago.

In this chapter, the reading selections are about active seniors. Pay attention to the language and ideas as you read. This will help you with the writing assignment later in this chapter.

Reading 1 is from a health newsletter. It is about what people can do to stay healthy as they get older. Before you read, talk to a classmate and answer these questions.

- What is one thing a person can do to live a long life?
- Can a person's attitude help him or her live longer?

Reading 1: Five Tips for Healthy Aging

1. Get **regular physical exercise.** Walk every day.
2. Get **mental exercise** too. Read, take a class, learn a language.
3. **Take care of your health.** Visit your doctor **regularly.**
4. Stay **active** socially. Talk to your friends. Visit your family.
5. Have a good **attitude.** Be **positive.**

                    —*Health Connections*

1. In "Five Tips for Healthy Aging" you read five **tips** and an **example** for each tip. Put a straight line under each tip. Put a wavy line under each example.

   Example: 1. Get regular physical exercise. Walk every day.

2. You will read some more examples below. Which tip for healthy aging do these people follow?

   a. Sally telephones her son every week. ___4___

   b. Emma walks with her dog. _____

   c. Jean and Jim play cards with their neighbors. _____

   d. Barbara feels good about her life. _____

   e. Knud is taking a Japanese cooking class. _____

   f. Tom has an appointment with his doctor next week. _____

3. Choose one of these:

   a. Write a short letter to someone you know who is over fifty-five. This person is not physically active or mentally active. Give this person three tips on healthy aging.

   b. Write your own plan to stay healthy as you age.

   _____

   _____

   _____

   _____

   _____

   _____

   _____

   _____

   _____

Reading 2 is a true story about a man who entered the longest bicycle race in the history of Sweden. Everyone believed he was too old to enter the race. Before you read, talk to a classmate and answer these questions:

- Have you ever watched a bicycle race?

- Do you know someone who rides in bicycle races?

- What must a person do or be to do well in a bicycle race?

Reading 2: Supergrandpa

Gustaf Håkansson was a 66-year-old Swede. His hair and beard were white. When he smiled, his face had many wrinkles. He looked like an old man, but he didn't feel old and he didn't act old. He stayed **active** by riding his bicycle everywhere in town. One day he read about the Tour of Sweden, a bicycle race. It was a long race and took many days. Everyone thought Gustaf was too old to enter the race. But Gustaf was **determined**.

He started the race several days before it began. He rode day and night. He slept in parks. As he rode, people shouted, "Look! Supergrandpa! Good luck, Supergrandpa!" The younger racers passed Gustaf. But while they slept at night, Gustaf continued to ride. On the seventh day, Gustaf rode to the finish line—before everyone. He won the race. He became a national hero. His example made other people feel young, **healthy,** and happy. He showed people in Sweden that you're never too old.

—David M. Schwartz

Supergrandpa's name in Swedish is *Stålfarfar*. It means "Steel Grandfather."

1. Gustaf entered a _____ race.

    a. bicycle

    b. car

    c. running

2. People believed Gustaf was_____.

    a. going to win

    b. too slow

    c. too old

3. Gustaf finished the race _____.

   a. last   b. first   c. after everyone else

4. Use the paragraph frame from "Supergrandpa" to write about someone you know. Change or add words if you like. Share what you write with a classmate.

   (1)_____ is a(n) (2)_____.

   S/he (3)_____ every (4)_____

   and (5)_____. At (6)_____

   s/he (7)_____. S/he doesn't (8)_____,

   but s/he (9)_____. Last (10)_____

   s/he (11)_____. S/he says (12)_____.

   Next (13)_____ s/he (14) _____.

   (15)_____!

ACADEMIC POWER STRATEGY

Be an active learner to learn and remember more. Good students are responsible learners. They are successful in their classes. Here are three things you can do to be an active learner.

Tips for Becoming an Active Learner

1. Be prepared for class. Have everything you need. Bring your books, notebooks, paper, and pens to class.

2. Study with a friend. Find a study buddy. Work together.

3. When you don't understand, ask the teacher questions. The teacher wants to help you learn.

Apply the Strategy

Make an Active Learner Plan. Write three things you will do to become a more active learner:

1. _____

2. _____

3. _____

Talk about your Active Learning Plan with a classmate. Review it in two weeks to see if you are following your own tips.

FROM READING TO WRITING

∙∙

◆ **Getting Ready to Write**

Choose a Topic

In this chapter, you will write about an active older person you know. Choose a person who is active in one of the following ways:

- The person is physically active.

- The person is mentally active.

Write your topic here:

I will write about _____

_____

_____

_____

_____

Here are some instructions for writing:

**Instructions for Writing About
An Active Senior**

1. Begin with a sentence that tells the person's name and how this person is active.

Here are some examples of first sentences from paragraphs in this chapter:

- *Doc Sinclair is an 81-year-old athlete.*

- *Uncle George is the most active member in my family.*

2. Give examples of activities the person does.

- *He gets up every morning at 4:00 A.M. and runs seven miles.*

- *When Uncle George is home, he plays tennis every day.*

3. Make sure all your sentences tell about the person you're describing.

Study a Student Example

Before you begin, read this paragraph by a community college student. Use active reading strategies.

Uncle George

Uncle George is the most active member in my family. And he's the oldest. He turned 77 on his last birthday in May. In the winter, he walks on snowshoes to his cabin in the mountains. In the summer he drives from southern California to Oregon and Washington to visit his children. When Uncle George is home, he plays tennis every day. I played tennis with him last week. I am fifty years younger than my uncle, but guess who won?

1. Write two examples the writer uses to show that Uncle George is active:

   a. _____

   b. _____

2. What is one thing you noticed and liked about the writing?

   _____

   _____

   _____

3. What is one question or suggestion you have?

   _____

   _____

Write

Now write your own paragraph about an active senior. Use the topic you chose on page 55. Review what you have learned in this chapter. You may want to use the writing you began in the Freewrite activity.

After You Write

Revise

First, have someone look at the ideas in your writing. Give your finished paragraph to a classmate. Your classmate will complete these statements.

1. The paragraph is about this active person:

   _____

2. These are ways the person is active:

   a. _____

   b. _____

3. The writer could add or change this to improve the paragraph:

   _____

   _____

Make changes to improve the ideas in your writing.

Edit

Now have someone check your writing for organization and language. Give your revised paragraph to a classmate. Your classmate will answer these questions:

1. Does the first sentence introduce the person?   Yes   No

2. Are all of the sentences in the paragraph about this person?
   Yes   No

   If the answer is no, which sentence isn't about this person?

   _____

3. Does the writer use capital letters correctly?   Yes   No

   If the answer is no, which words should be corrected?

   _____

4. Are there any language mistakes? (Please write them here.)
   Yes   No

   _____

Make corrections to your writing.

PUTTING IT ALL TOGETHER

◇ **Use What You Have Learned**

1. Write another paragraph about someone else you know or a famous person. This person can be active mentally or physically. Try to write more quickly this time.

2. Talk or write more about the quotation you read at the beginning of this chapter. Here are some more lines from Pablo Neruda's poem "Ode to Age":

> I don't believe in age.
>
> All old people
>
> carry
>
> in their eyes
>
> a child . . .

Test-Taking Tip

Use flashcards to help you study for tests. Flashcards are index cards on which you write important information you want to study. For example, to study important words or ideas for a test, write a word or a question on one side of the flashcard and the definition or the answer to the question on the other side of the card. Use these flashcards to test yourself whenever and wherever you have some free time.

CHECK YOUR PROGRESS

On a scale of 1 to 5, rate how well you have mastered the goals set at the beginning of the chapter:

1 2 3 4 5   write a paragraph about an active senior you know.

1 2 3 4 5   learn parts of speech to write more correct sentences.

1 2 3 4 5   learn how to read actively in order to improve your writing.

1 2 3 4 5   make an Active Learner Plan.

1 2 3 4 5   practice using rules of capitalization.

If you've given yourself a 3 or lower on any of these goals:

- visit the *Tapestry* web site for additional practice.
- ask your instructor for extra help.
- review the sections of the chapter that you found difficult.
- work with a partner or study group to further your progress.

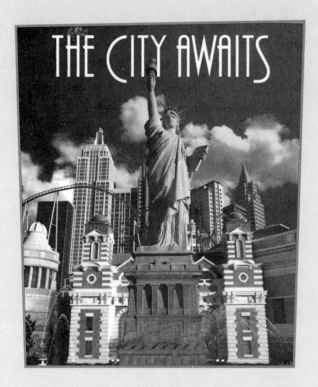

THE CITY AWAITS

"When you write about a place,
try to draw the best out of it."

—William Zinsser

Where was the photo taken? How do you know?

What does the quotation mean?

When you read about a place, what do you want to learn?

NEW YORK–NEW YORK IN LAS VEGAS

Where have you been? Where do you want to go? This chapter is about places to visit. Some people travel far to visit interesting places. Other people visit interesting places close to home. You will read and think about places to visit. Then you will write about a place that interests you.

Setting Goals

In this chapter you will:

◈ write about a place to visit.

In order to do this, you will:

◈ learn the difference between facts and opinions.

◈ use strong adjectives to help the reader "see" what you describe.

◈ learn about the library to gather information for your writing.

◈ read about two places to visit to help you prepare for writing.

◈ review the use of prepositions.

<table>
<tr><td colspan="2"></td></tr>
</table>

Getting Started

Do you like the city or the country? Do you like places where the weather is warm? Do you like theme parks? In Column 1, write the kinds of places you like to visit. In Column 2, write the names of specific places you know.

Column 1: Some Kinds of Places You Like to Visit	Column 2: Names of Specific Places You Know
big cities	New York City, New York Mexico City, Mexico Tokyo, Japan

> A vacation is a trip when you take twice the clothes and half the money you need.
>
> —ANONYMOUS

MEETING THE TOPIC

Talk with a Partner

LANGUAGE LEARNING STRATEGY

Use strong adjectives to help the reader "see" what you are writing about. In Chapter 3, you learned that adjectives are words that describe. Strong adjectives will make your writing clear. Strong adjectives are specific. They help the reader see, hear, smell, or feel what the writer is describing. General adjectives are vague. They do not give a picture of what the writer is describing. Read the following examples of strong and general adjectives:

STRONG ADJECTIVES ARE	GENERAL ADJECTIVES ARE
• specific	• vague
• exact	• imprecise
• clear	• unclear

scenic	fine
snow-capped	nice
lovely	average
unforgettable	

Collect strong adjectives in your Writer's Portfolio.

Apply the Strategy

Look at these photos of different places. With a partner, match adjectives to places. Add more adjectives if you can.

tropical   crowded   dramatic   busy   unforgettable

noisy   quiet   peaceful   beautiful

a.

b.

c.

d.

e.

f.

Freewrite

Freewrite about a place to visit. It should be a place you know well. Write everything you know about this place. Answer any of the following questions to begin. Then write some other things you know about this place. Use as many strong adjectives as you can.

The two most popular National Parks in the United States are the Blue Ridge Parkway (in North Carolina and Virginia) and the Golden Gate National Recreation Area (in California).

- Where is it?
- How do you know it?
- What do you see there?
- Whom do you see there?
- What do you hear, smell, and feel when you're there?

Write for ten minutes. You will add to this writing throughout the chapter. You may choose to use it for the assignment later.

LANGUAGE LEARNING STRATEGY

Learn the difference between facts and opinions. This will help you become a better reader. It will also help you decide what to include in your writing.

- A **fact** is true for all people. You want to use lots of facts when you include information in your writing.

- An **opinion** expresses a preference or a feeling and is not true for all people. Opinions make your writing personal.

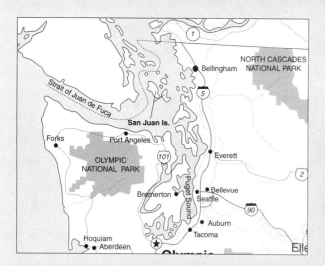

Read these examples about the San Juan Islands.

Fact: *The San Juan Islands are between the United States and Canada.*

Opinion: *The weather in the San Juan Islands is perfect.*

Apply the Strategy

Read the following paragraph about the San Juan Islands. Underline **facts** and write a wavy line under **opinions**.

Many people visit the San Juan Islands during the summer. Visitors can take a ferry, seaplane, charter boat, or airplane to visit the islands. Ferries are the most comfortable way to go. The San Juan Islands are beautiful. You can really relax there.

Now reread your freewrite. Underline facts. Can you add any facts? If you find an opinion, put a wavy line under it. If you don't find an opinion, add one.

TUNING IN: "What's So Special About Las Vegas?"

© CNN

The video you will watch shows some new places to visit in Las Vegas. You will read about one of these resorts later in the chapter. As you watch the video, think about whether you would like to visit one of these places. Then answer the questions.

1. Las Vegas has 104,000

   a. hotels.

   b. hotel rooms.

   c. hotel swimming pools.

2. There are three new mega-resorts in Las Vegas. What's a mega-resort?

   a. an airport

   b. a shopping center

   c. a huge hotel

3. What can a visitor find at New York–New York?

   a. Lady Liberty

   b. a beautiful view

   c. a famous magician

4. What can a visitor find at the Stratosphere?

   a. Lady Liberty

   b. a beautiful view

   c. a famous magician

5. What can a visitor find at Monte Carlo?

   a. Lady Liberty

   b. a beautiful view

   c. a famous magician

6. Would you like to visit Las Vegas? Why or why not?

   _____

   _____

   _____

EXPANDING YOUR LANGUAGE

Vocabulary Check

These words and expressions will help you with the writing for this chapter. Check those that you know. Work with a partner. Write the definitions of new words and use them in a sentence in the Vocabulary Section of your Writer's Portfolio.

_____ acre	_____ sand dune
_____ colorful	_____ skyline
_____ geography	_____ stunning
_____ landmark	_____ tower over
_____ local	_____ tropical
_____ re-create	_____ variety

Vocabulary Building

1. Review the definitions of words and expressions from the Vocabulary Check. Read the sentences and check the correct answer.

   a. You can find **sand dunes** at the beach and in the desert. They are

      _____ hills of sand.

      _____ holes in sand.

      _____ sand animals.

b. When you find a **variety** of trees, you find

_____ one kind.

_____ none.

_____ different kinds.

c. **Geography** is the study of

_____ the earth's surface.

_____ the earth's animals.

_____ the earth's people.

d. **Tropical** weather is

_____ icy.

_____ cold.

_____ warm.

e. The playground covers an **acre**. An **acre** is a

_____ measure of land.

_____ basketball court.

_____ tennis court.

f. The **local** museum is

_____ far away.

_____ nearby.

_____ overseas.

g. The **colorful** gardens in the park have

_____ many colors.

_____ no color.

_____ one color.

2. Write answers to these questions using the words in parentheses.

a. Which building, structure, or tree do you often see in your community? Describe what it looks like and where it is located. (**landmark**)

_____

_____

_____

b. What is the most memorable, beautiful, or unforgettable sight you've seen? (**stunning**)

_____

_____

_____

c. What is the tallest building or mountain you have visited? Where is it, and what is nearby? (**tower over**)

_____

_____

_____

3. Draw a skyline you remember well. It can be from a city or from the country. If you can't remember a skyline you've seen, draw the skyline of a famous city or mountain or range of mountains. (Look at some pictures if you like.)

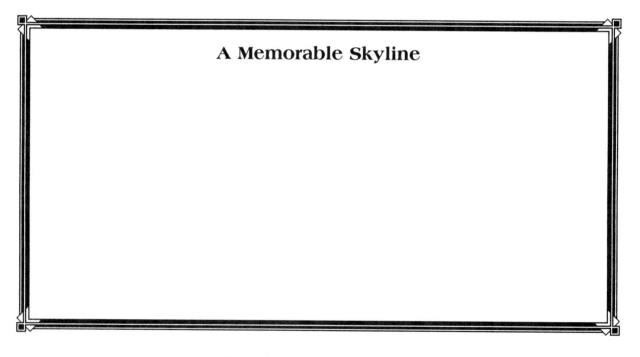

A Memorable Skyline

Write about your drawing. Explain what it is, where it is, and what you have tried to show in it.

_____

_____

_____

Grammar You Can Use: Prepositions

Prepositions show relationships between objects and ideas. Writers use prepositions to describe where a place is located and what they find in that place. You will want to include prepositions when you write about a place to visit. Review this list of prepositions. Then read the paragraph.

next to	behind
far from	around
above	across from
below	in the middle of
in front of	through

The Library of Heilongjoang Province

The Library of Heilongjoang Province is my favorite place to visit. It is one of many famous places to see in Harbin in northeast China. The library is **in the middle of** the city. It has six tall columns **in front of** the entrance. There is a balcony **above** the columns. The balcony is **next to** two reading rooms. Visitors can walk **through** a clock tower on the fifth floor. I walked **around** the library often. I didn't have much time to study.

—Dora M. Chin

Practice using prepositions. Write a letter to a friend about a place in your school or community. If you like, use the freewrite you began earlier. Add prepositions.

Dear _____,

_____

_____

_____

_____

_____

_____

_____

_____

Sincerely,

_____

READING FOR WRITING

You will read about two places to visit. When you read another person's writing, you learn ideas about the topic. You also learn ways to express and organize your own ideas for writing.

Reading 1 is about a park in San Francisco, California. Before you read, think about a park you like to visit. Talk to a classmate and answer these questions.

- What do you see and do at the park?

- What is your favorite city park? Why?

- What makes a city park great?

Reading 1: Golden Gate Park

Are you ready to see the *real* San Francisco? Grab a skateboard. Hop on a bike. Take a kite and a baseball mitt and go to Golden Gate Park. There are many things to do here. You won't want to leave. Golden Gate Park is huge. It has 1,017 **acres** of trees, grass, hiking paths, bike trails, baseball fields, basketball courts, a golf course, tennis courts, playgrounds, ponds, museums, and outdoor concert spaces. Don't miss the large Children's Playground. You can climb on bars, hang from rings, and dig in sand. Can you believe that this park was once a huge **sand dune**? It was called the Great Sand Wastes. Many people believed a park could never be built here. They were wrong!

1. The writer likes Golden Gate Park because

   a. there are many things to do.

   b. there is a lot of sand.

   c. it is crowded.

2. A visitor can find these in Golden Gate Park:

   a. bike trails.

   b. playgrounds.

   c. both of these.

3. A visitor can do these activities in Golden Gate Park:

   a. play tennis.

   b. go shopping.

   c. swim.

4. Write three facts and two opinions from "Golden Gate Park."

FACTS	OPINIONS
•	•
•	•
•	

Reading 2 is about a casino in Las Vegas, Nevada. Before you read, answer these questions with a classmate.

- If you have never been to Las Vegas, what do you know about it? If you have visited Las Vegas, what do you remember?

- A casino is a large hall where people come for entertainment. Have you ever visited a casino? Where?

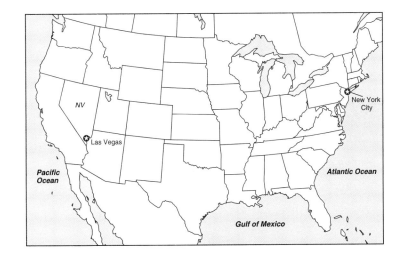

Reading 2: Which New York Do You Want to Visit?

New York–New York Hotel & Casino in Las Vegas, the Greatest City in Las Vegas, **re-creates** the very best of the Big Apple. It **towers over** the Las Vegas Strip and offers the sights, sounds, and energy of New York. It has **stunning** re-creations of the city's most famous **landmarks**. You can see the Manhattan **skyline**, the Brooklyn Bridge, Times Square, and the Statue of

Liberty. This is the tallest hotel in Nevada, and it has fantastic views. Visit Central Park and play some games. Watch a show with New York performers. Dance and sing at the Empire Bar. Kids of all ages enjoy the Coney Island Emporium, which combines old-fashioned roller coasters with high-tech video games. Master chefs prepare delicious Italian, Chinese, and American food. Call now and make a plan to visit.

1. The Big Apple is in
   a. Las Vegas, Nevada.
   b. New York.
   c. Chicago.

2. New York–New York is a re-creation of
   a. Golden Gate Park.
   b. San Francisco.
   c. New York City.

3. You can find a re-creation of this bridge at New York–New York:
   a. the Golden Gate Bridge.
   b. the Brooklyn Bridge.
   c. the London Bridge.

4. Write a letter to a friend. Tell your friend three facts about New York–New York. Then write your opinion of this place.

Dear _____,

_____

_____

_____

_____

_____

_____

_____

Sincerely,

_____

FROM READING TO WRITING

Getting Ready to Write

Choose a Topic

In this chapter, you are going to write about a place to visit. Choose one of these kinds of places:

- a place to visit in your native country
- a place that you want to visit in the future
- a place in Canada or the United States
- a place that is not well-known
- a popular place for tourists

Choose your topic and write it here: *I will write about* _____

_____.

Here are some instructions for writing:

Instructions for Writing About a Place to Visit

1. Begin with the **name and/or location of the place.** Here are some examples from this chapter:

   - *The Library of Heilongjoang Province is my favorite place to visit.*
   - *Many people visit the San Juan Islands during the summer.*
   - *New York–New York Hotel & Casino in Las Vegas, the Greatest City in Las Vegas . . .*

2. Describe **what you can see** and **what you can do** in this place. Here are some examples from this chapter:

   - *You can climb on bars, hang from rings, and dig in sand.*
   - *You can see the Manhattan skyline, the Brooklyn Bridge, Times Square, and the Statue of Liberty.*

3. **Make your writing interesting** to read. Communicate your personality through your writing. (Writers call this **voice.**) One way to do this is to "speak" directly to the reader. Look at these examples:

   - *Grab a skateboard. Hop on a bike.*
   - *Call now and make a plan to visit.*

Most popular U.S. cities for foreign visitors each year:
New York, 4.3 million
Los Angeles: 3.1 million
San Francisco: 2.65 million

ACADEMIC POWER STRATEGY

Learn about the library to gather information for your writing. You will want to know where to find facts when writing about a place. The school or local library can help you get information. Visit the library. Take a tour and learn how to use its resources.

Apply the Strategy

Go to the library and make yourself a fact-finding guide. Write the names of places in the library where you can find information about places. As you make this guide for yourself, look for facts about the topic of your writing. Add a map or a picture or a diagram if you find one at the library.

Library Fact-Finding Guide:
Where to Find Information About Places

Name of Library: _____

Address of Library: _____

Name of Librarian: _____

Maps/Atlases	Encyclopedias
Room _____	Room _____
Section _____	Section _____
Shelf or Station _____	Shelf or Station _____
Title of Book or Computer Address _____	Title of Book or Computer Address _____
Facts About My Topic _____	Facts About My Topic _____

Picture Books	Travel Guides
Room _____	Room _____
Section _____	Section _____
Shelf or Station _____	Shelf or Station _____
Title of Book or Computer Address _____	Title of Book or Computer Address _____
Facts About My Topic _____	Facts About My Topic _____

Computers

Room ——————————————————————

Section ————————————————————

Shelf or Station ——————————————

Title of Book or Computer Address ——————

Facts About My Topic —————————

Dictionaries

Room ——————————————————————

Section ————————————————————

Shelf or Station ——————————————

Title of Book or Computer Address ——————

Facts About My Topic —————————

Video Library

Room ——————————————————————

Section ————————————————————

Shelf or Station ——————————————

Title of Book or Computer Address ——————

Facts About My Topic —————————

Audio Library

Room ——————————————————————

Section ————————————————————

Shelf or Station ——————————————

Title of Book or Computer Address ——————

Facts About My Topic —————————

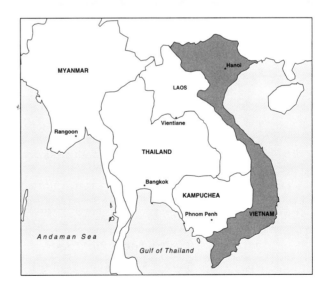

Study a Student Example

Before you write, read this paragraph written by a student.

My Hometown

Dalat, located in the southern part of Vietnam, is a lovely place to visit. It's on a hill so there are scenic views of mountains, valleys, and waterfalls.

There is a big lake in the middle of the valley. It is called "Lamenting Lake." There are lots of activities around the lake. People ride boats and enjoy the fresh air and clear water. The weather is comfortable in Dalat all year. It never gets too hot or too cold. Many people spend their vacation in Dalat. It's my hometown and I will never forget it.

—Phuong Lu

1. What are two things a visitor can do in Dalat?

   a. _____

   b. _____

2. What is one thing you noticed and liked about Phuong's writing?

   _____

   _____

   _____

3. What is one question or suggestion you have?

   _____

   _____

   _____

Write

Now write about the place to visit that you chose in the exercise on page 73. Review what you have learned in this chapter and use the writing you've already done.

After You Write

Revise

First, have someone look at the ideas in your writing. Give your finished paragraph to a classmate. Your classmate will complete these statements.

1. The paragraph is about this place to visit:

   _____

   _____

2. These are things you can see there:

   a. _____

   b. _____

3. These are things you can do there:

   a. _____

   b. _____

4. The writer gives an opinion or speaks directly to the reader in this sentence:

   _____

   _____

5. The writer can add or change this to improve the paragraph:

   _____

   _____

   _____

Make changes to improve the ideas in your writing.

Edit

Now have someone check your writing for organization and language. Give your revised paragraph to a classmate. Your classmate will answer these questions.

1. Does the first sentence tell the name of the place?   Yes   No

2. Are all of the sentences in the paragraph about this place?
   Yes   No

   If the answer is no, which sentence isn't about this place?

   _____

   _____

In California, you can easily visit the tallest mountain in the continental U.S., Mt. Whitney (14,494 feet), and the lowest point, Death Valley (282 feet below sea level), in one day. They are only 60 miles apart!

3. Does the writer use prepositions to show the relationship between objects or landmarks or places to visit?   Yes   No

   If the answer is no, what can the writer add or change?

   _____

   _____

4. Are there any language mistakes? (Please write them here.)
   Yes   No

   _____

   _____

Make corrections to your writing.

PUTTING IT ALL TOGETHER

Use What You Have Learned

1. Write a travel brochure about another place to visit. Include facts and opinions that will attract lots of people.

2. Design a poster for a local place to visit. Gather some facts by talking to people in the community. Make a presentation to your class.

Test-Taking Tip

Make sure you are physically prepared for tests. The night before a test, be sure to get a good night's sleep. It is hard to concentrate when you feel tired. It is also important to eat at least a light breakfast the day of the test—you cannot do your best work on an empty stomach.

CHECK YOUR PROGRESS

On a scale of 1 to 5, rate how well you have mastered the goals set at the beginning of the chapter:

1 2 3 4 5   write about a place to visit.

1 2 3 4 5   learn the difference between facts and opinions.

1 2 3 4 5   use strong adjectives to help the reader "see" what you describe.

1 2 3 4 5   learn about the library to gather information for your writing.

1 2 3 4 5   review the use of prepositions.

If you've given yourself a 3 or lower on any of these goals:

- visit the *Tapestry* web site for additional practice.
- ask your instructor for extra help.
- review the sections of the chapter that you found difficult.
- work with a partner or study group to further your progress.

"Adolescence is unlike any other period in life."

—Anthony Wolf

H ow old is the person in the photo?

Is she a child or an adult?

Do you agree with the quotation? Why or why not?

TEENAGERS

Do you remember when you were a teenager? Did you look odd or do strange things? Some people believe that teenagers look odd. And some adults think teenagers do strange things. Do you know some teenagers who do not look odd and who do normal things? In this chapter, you will read and think about teenagers today, then you will write about a teenager you know.

Setting Goals

In this chapter you will learn how to:

◈ write a paragraph about a teenager you know.

In order to do this, you will:

◈ continue to learn the parts of speech to write correct sentences.

◈ learn how to tell the difference between general and specific ideas in sentences in order to write strong paragraphs.

◈ learn about cultural differences in order to appreciate where you are living and where your classmates come from.

◈ read two articles about teenagers to prepare for writing.

◈ practice using the past habitual verb tense to write about the past.

Getting Started

Think of a teenager you know. If you don't know any teenagers personally, think of a teenager from a movie or TV show. What makes teenagers different than children? What makes them different than adults? Think about how the person you know looks, the language he or she uses, and what this person does. Record some ideas about this teenager in the chart below. Then discuss these ideas with a classmate.

	A Teenager I Know
What he/she looks like	
What he/she says	
What he/she does	

MEETING THE TOPIC

Talk with a Partner

Work with a classmate and match the photos to the quotes. There is more than one way to match. Explain your matches.

1. _____ Teresa: "I think girls can do almost anything they want."

2. _____ Alex: "I work hard at school. When it's vacation, I love to play video games."

3. _____ Maureen: "I hated being twelve. It's too young. Now I'm thirteen, and I'm much happier."

4. _____ Peter: "I want to be a singer or an actor. I don't want to be a professional athlete. Athletes have too much stress."

5. _____ Sarah: "I'm planning to teach and travel all over the world. And I'm going to learn lots of languages, too."

6. _____ Morgan: "There's too much to do and not enough time. I have school, homework, friends, parties, and family. I'm totally stressed out!"

a.

b.

c.

d.

e.

f.

Ask and answer these questions:

- When does a person become a teenager?
- When does "teenagehood" end?
- What is your opinion of teenagers in the U.S. and Canada?
- Are teenagers different in different parts of the world?
- Do you remember some things you did when you were a teenager?

◈ **Freewrite**

Freewrite about a teenager you know. If you don't know a teenager, write about a teenager from a movie or a TV show. Answer any of these questions to begin. Then write your own ideas.

- Who is this teenager?
- How do you know this person?
- How old is this teenager?

- What does he or she look like?
- What does the teenager do?
- Do you think this person is a typical teenager?

Write for as long as you can. Write as much as you can. You will use this writing later.

◆ Grammar You Can Use: Past Habitual Tense

> **What is a favorite activity for most teenagers? Going to the movies.**

Writers use the expression *used to* in order to describe actions they did in the past on a regular basis. They were "past habits." Use this verb tense when something happened repeatedly in the past. Read these examples:

> *Johnetta **used to** listen to music all day every day.*
> *My neighbors and I **used to** deliver newspapers.*
> *The student **used to** take the bus to school. Now she drives a car.*

To form the past habitual tense, write used to + the simple form of the verb. Practice using this expression by answering these questions about yourself when you were a teenager.

1. What did you do in your free time?

   _____

   _____

2. What did you like to eat?

   _____

   _____

3. Which places did you visit regularly?

   _____

   _____

4. Who did you spend time with?

   _____

   _____

TUNING IN: "Superteen"

The video in this chapter is about a teenager who is working like an adult. Read the questions, watch the video, and then answer the questions. Watch the video several times to check your answers.

© CNN

1. How old is Sean?

   a. fourteen   b. fifteen   c. sixteen

2. What is he doing at the computer show?

   a. selling computers

   b. selling computer software

   c. playing on the microphone

3. As an employee, what is something Sean can do?

   a. go to school

   b. work after 11 P.M.

   c. work more than 8 hours a day

4. What does Sean do when he's not at computer shows?

   a. looks for a job

   b. acts in television shows

   c. studies at a community college

5. What is Sean planning to do right after he leaves the computer show?

   a. study for a final exam

   b. go home to sleep

   c. look for a job in Silicon Valley

LANGUAGE LEARNING STRATEGY

Learn how to tell the difference between general and specific ideas in sentences. Good writers begin paragraphs with one <u>general</u> sentence, often called the <u>topic sentence</u>. Then they use specific ideas to explain and support the first sentence. Learning the difference between general and specific ideas will help you develop strong paragraphs. Follow these guidelines to tell the difference between general and specific ideas:

- Ideas are general or specific in **relation to each other.** Always read the sentences before and after to tell if an idea is general or specific.
- A **general idea** is true for a group of people or things:
     Teenagers are different today.
- A **specific idea** is true for only a few people or one person:
     Joshua, sixteen, wears only black clothes and works in a bookstore.

(continued on next page)

Apply the Strategy

1. Read the sentences below. Check "general" or "specific" in the column next to each sentence.

	General	Specific
(a) Friends are everything to a teenager.	_____	_____
(b) Teenagers no longer want to spend time with parents or brothers or sisters.	_____	_____
(c) They only want to be with their friends.	_____	_____
(d) Jordan, a tenth-grader at the local high school, is a typical teenager.	_____	_____
(e) He spends all of his free time with his friends.	_____	_____
(f) Their names are Jeremy, John, and Jason.	_____	_____
(g) They call themselves the "J Group."	_____	_____

2. Now write your own paragraph about someone you know. Include at least six sentences. Make the first two sentences general, the next three specific, and the last sentence general.

_____

_____

_____

_____

_____

_____

EXPANDING YOUR LANGUAGE

◆**Vocabulary Check**

The following words and expressions will help you with the reading and writing in this chapter. Which ones do you know? Check them. Work with a partner. Learn the definitions of new words and add them to the Vocabulary Section of your Writer's Portfolio.

_____ adolescence   _____ be motivated to
                                              (do something)
_____ be acceptable

_____ be respectful (of someone)   _____ harsh punishment

_____ be stressed (out)   _____ independent

_____ behave   _____ treat someone (adverb)

_____ feel a lot of pressure   _____ typical

_____ feel free

Vocabulary Building

1. Use words and expressions from the Vocabulary Check to write about the teenagers in the photos on page 83. Use their names in complete sentences to answer the questions.

    Here are the names: Teresa Alex Maureen Peter Sarah Morgan

    a. Which teenager **feels a lot of pressure?**

    _____

    _____

    b. Which teenager does not want **to feel a lot of pressure?**

    _____

    _____

    c. Who believes that **it is acceptable** for men and women to have the same jobs?

    _____

    _____

    d. Which two teenagers are **motivated to be successful** in the future?

    _____

    _____

e. *Challenge Questions:* Is there something **typical** about these teenagers? What does a **typical** teenager do? What does a **typical** teenager want for the future?

_____

_____

_____

2. Match the expression from the Vocabulary Check in Column 1 to the example in Column 2.

COLUMN 1: EXPRESSIONS	COLUMN 2: EXAMPLES
Anna **feels a lot of pressure.**	She does anything she wants any time she wants.
Megan received **harsh punishment.**	She does all her homework and pays attention in class because she wants to get good grades.
Janie **feels free.**	She is grounded for a month.
Laurie **is respectful.**	She can't go to dances if she doesn't get good grades.
Pia is **motivated to do well in school.**	When she meets people, she shakes their hands and looks at them.

3. Teenagers often follow popular trends. These trends decide what they buy, what they wear, how they style their hair, or what they say. Write two trends you notice among teenagers today. Then write two trends that were popular when you were a teenager.

POPULAR TEENAGE TRENDS TODAY	TRENDS WHEN I WAS A TEENAGER
a. _____	a. _____
_____	_____
b. _____	b. _____
_____	_____

LANGUAGE LEARNING STRATEGY

Learn the parts of speech and know how to use them. In Chapter 3 you learned that all words in English belong to a group. You studied the following parts of speech: nouns, pronouns, verbs, and adjectives. In this chapter you will learn about these four parts of speech:

✻ **adverb** (a word which tells how, when, where, why, how often, and how much):

> *slowly, carefully, fast, regularly, well*
>
> *The young man moves **slowly** and **carefully**. He thinks **quickly** and **clearly**.*

✻ **preposition** (word or group of words that shows how two objects or ideas are related):

> *after, from, into, beside, along*
>
> *The teenagers sit in the park **beside** the garden **after** school. They visit **with** friends.*

(See Chapter 4 for more on prepositions.)

✻ **conjunction** (connects words or groups of words):

> *and, or, but*
>
> *Jenni exercises in front of TV **and** next to the radio. She doesn't exercise on Saturday **or** Sunday.*

✻ **interjection** (word or phrase to express surprise or strong emotion):

> *Wow! What a surprise! Oh no! Congratulations!*
>
> **She did it!** She finished her homework! **Great!**

Apply the Strategy

1. Complete the following paragraph. Use the part of speech indicated. Choose from the lists below.

Prepositions	Conjunctions	Adverbs	Interjection
across	but	joyfully	What a pleasure
in	and	regularly	
at	although	easily	
		now	

Alex is a sixteen-year-old musician. He plays the piano (preposition) 1. _____ home (conjunction) 2. _____ the saxophone (preposition) 3. _____ school. He also plays the drums when he visits his friend who lives (preposition) 4. _____

(continued on next page)

the street. He studied the violin when he was ten, (conjunction)

5. _____ he doesn't play it (adverb) 6. _____.

(conjunction) 7. _____ he doesn't take music

lessons, he plays (adverb) 8. _____. He plays all

the instruments (adverb) 9. _____ (conjunction)

10. _____ (adverb) 11. _____.

(interjection) 12. _____ to listen to Alex play!

2. With a partner, write a paragraph about a famous teenager. Choose a TV or movie star. Add the missing parts of speech to complete the paragraph. You can make the sentences longer (or shorter).

(Noun) 1. _____ (verb) 2. _____

a (adjective) 3. _____ (noun) 4. _____.

(Pronoun) 5. _____ (verb) 6. _____

every (noun) 7. _____. (Pronoun) 8. _____

also (verb) 9. _____. (Noun) 10. _____

doesn't (verb) 11. _____. (Pronoun) 12. _____

says (pronoun) 13. _____ (verb) 14. _____.

I think (noun) 15. _____ (verb) 16. _____

(adjective) 17. _____.

READING FOR WRITING

You will read two articles about teenagers. The first selection is about a specific teenager, and the second is about teenagers in general. The reading will help you with the language and ideas for your writing assignment in this chapter.

Reading 1 is about a typical teenager. Before you read, talk to a classmate and answer these questions:

- Do you think being a teenager is easy or difficult? Why?
- What was easy when you were a teenager? What was difficult?

Reading 1: Thirteen Is Hard

Carlos Quintana is thirteen years old. He lives in New York City and rides the subway to school. He studies hard because he wants to go to a good college. He plans to be a doctor. Carlos says that **he feels a lot of pressure** at his age. First, there is **pressure** at school. Then there is **pressure** to have friends and to look cool. "You have to wear the right clothes and the right shoes," Carlos says. "Thirteen is a hard age. It's very hard."

1. These sentences say the **opposite** of what is true for Carlos. Correct them by writing true sentences about Carlos.

   a. Carlos is not motivated to do well in school.

   _____

   _____

   b. Carlos is relaxed about school.

   _____

   _____

   c. Carlos doesn't care about what he wears.

   _____

   _____

Three to four million children will be turning thirteen every year until 2010.

d. Carlos believes that it's easy to be thirteen.

_____

_____

2. Use the paragraph frame from "Thirteen Is Hard" to write about a teenager you know. Develop your freewrite from Meeting the Topic. Change or add words to make your writing true.

1. (Name)_____ is 2. _____

years old. S/he lives in 3. _____ and 4.

_____ to school. S/he 5. _____

in school because s/he wants 6._____. S/he plans

to be a 7. _____. 8. (Name)_____

says that s/he feels 9. _____. First there is 10.

_____. Then there is 11. _____

"You have to 12. _____," 13. (Name)_____

says. "14. _____."

Reading 2 is about how teenagers today are different than teenagers in the past. Before you read, talk to a classmate and answer these questions:

- What do teenagers do today that they didn't do in the past?

- What do you think teenagers will do in the future that they don't do today?

Reading 2: Being a Teenager: It's Not the Way It Used to Be

Teenagers have really changed. They seem to **be less respectful** and more **independent** than teenagers in past generations. Did teenagers twenty years ago have pagers and cell phones? Definitely not. But parents have changed too. Parents behave differently with their children nowadays. Most parents do not treat their children **harshly. Harsh punishment** is clearly not as **acceptable** as it used to be. Today teenagers **feel freer** to do what they want to do. This can cause problems. It can separate parents and children. There are ways to bring parents and children together. Some communities have solutions to this problem. There are parent-child reading groups. Some clubs organize father-daughter activities. Schools encourage parents to be active in their child's education. The new teenager is different, but *not* impossible. Parents must try to communicate with their teenagers about their lives and interests. And they must **be respectful of their children.** Parents must learn a different kind of strength than their parents used.

—Anthony Wolf

1. How are teenagers different today from the way they used to be?

    a. They seem disrespectful.

    b. They are more independent.

    c. Both of these.

2. How are parents different today from the way they used to be?

    a. They treat their children less harshly.

    b. They treat their children more harshly.

    c. They feel freer.

3. What can parents do to be successful with teenagers today?

    a. They can treat their children more harshly.

    b. They can have pagers and cell phones.

    c. They can communicate with their children.

4. Think about how teenagers from Canada or the United States and your native culture spend their time. Fill in a Venn diagram showing what is similar and what is different. In A, write what teenagers from your native culture do. In B, write what teenagers from Canada or the United States do. In C, write about teenagers

from both cultures. Your writing in C will show what teenagers from two different cultures do. Look at some of these ideas to get started, then add your own ideas:

- *They go to movies with their parents.*
- *They help with housework.*
- *They do what their parents tell them to do.*
- *They take care of younger brothers and sisters.*
- *They have jobs to earn money to go shopping.*

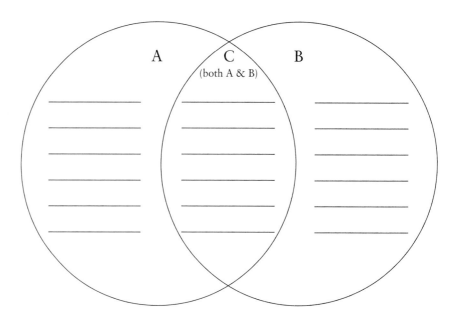

5. Write a paragraph about teenagers in two different cultures based on the Venn diagram from the previous exercise. Are teenagers in the two cultures mostly similar or mostly different?

_____

_____

_____

_____

_____

_____

_____

Early in the twenty-first century the population of America's teenagers will reach 30 million, more than at any other time since 1975.

ACADEMIC POWER STRATEGY

Learn about cultural differences in order to appreciate where you are living and where your classmates come from. You can learn a lot from your classmates. You can learn about languages, cultures, and different ways of solving problems. Working successfully with people from different cultures will help you succeed in school. Appreciating diversity will also prepare you for life and work after you complete your education.

Apply the Strategy

Find out about teenagers in other cultures. Interview three people from different cultures between the ages of thirteen and nineteen. Ask them to describe special events in their lives. (If this is not possible, interview three people of any age and culture. Ask them about their memories of being a teenager.) These could be formal family celebrations where young people become adults. *Quinceañera, Bar Mitzvah,* and *Bat Mitzvah* are examples of these kinds of events. Or you can ask them about everyday events. Learning to cook, getting one's driver's license, and moving away from home are also examples of important events in the life of a teenager. Share your completed chart with a classmate. Continue to learn about cultural differences as you study.

(continued on next page)

IMPORTANT EVENTS IN A TEENAGER'S LIFE	
Teenager's Name, Age, and Native Culture	Important Event(s)

Go back to the Academic Power Strategy in Chapter 3 on page 54. Review your Active Learner Plan. Are you meeting your goal? If your answer is yes, congratulations! If your answer is no, make a better plan or change the goal.

FROM READING TO WRITING

◄ **Getting Ready To Write**   **Choose a Topic**

This chapter's assignment is to write a paragraph about a teenager. You can write about:

- someone you know (from any culture) who is between the ages of thirteen and nineteen

- someone who is no longer a teenager (but describe this person when he or she was a teenager)

- someone who is a famous teenager (but who you know well enough to write about)

- yourself (if you are a teenager)

Choose your topic and write it here:

I will write about _____

_____

Here are some instructions for writing:

Instructions for Writing About a Teenager

1. Begin with a sentence that introduces the person. You can give the person's name and/or age and/or interests. The beginning of your paragraph should have general information. Here are examples of first sentences from this chapter:

   • *Carlos Quintana is thirteen years old.*

   • *Sixteen-year-old Maria wants to be an independent young woman.*

2. Describe activities the person does and interests the person has. Give examples of these. This part of your paragraph should have specific information. Here are examples from this chapter:

   • *He studies hard because he wants to go to a good college.*

   • *Maria wants to feel free, to go out with friends and have fun.*

3. Teenagers are interesting and different. Try to include information about what makes the person unique. Here are some examples:

   • *Carlos says that he feels a lot of pressure at his age.*

   • *Maria's values are very different from the traditional values of her parents.*

Study a Student Example

Before you write, read this paragraph by a student.

The Clash

Sixteen-year-old Maria wants to be an independent young woman. She wants to wear make-up. Her parents think she's too young. She should wait until college. Maria's friend, Hwang, wants to go to a party and stay out late. His parents want him home early. These are just a few of the conflicts between teenagers and their parents. If they are immigrants, the conflict is bigger. Teenagers learn new cultural values in this country. The values are very different from the traditional values of their parents. Maria's parents want her to cook and clean. They want Maria to keep the house neat and be respectful to her older brother. Her parents want her to be a traditional Korean woman. Maria doesn't want to cook or clean or stay at home. She wants a career. She wants to feel free, to go out with friends and have fun. The result is a clash between Maria and her parents.

—Ilene Chong

1. What three disagreements do Maria and her parents have?

   a. _____

   b. _____

   c. _____

2. The writer believes that conflicts between immigrant parents and teenagers are _____ than between nonimmigrant parents and teenagers.

   a. less serious

   b. more serious

   c. both of these

3. Many immigrant parents want their children to be

   a. modern.

   b. independent.

   c. traditional.

4. What is one thing you noticed and liked about the writing?

   _____

   _____

   _____

5. What is one question or suggestion you have?

   _____

   _____

   _____

Write

Now write your own paragraph. Review what you have learned about writing about teenagers. Use the topic you chose on page 96, and any writing you've already begun from any part of this chapter.

After You Write

Revise

First, have someone look at the ideas in your writing. Give your finished paragraph to a classmate. Your classmate will complete these statements:

1. The paragraph is about this teenager:

   _____

2. These are some interests the teenager has:

   a. _____

   b. _____

   c. _____

3. The teenager is unique in this way:

   _____

   _____

   _____

4. The writer could add or change this to improve the paragraph:

   _____

   _____

   _____

Make changes to improve your writing.

Edit

Now have someone check your writing for organization and language. Give your revised paragraph to a classmate. Your classmate will answer these questions.

1. Does the first sentence introduce the person?   Yes   No

2. Does the writer begin with general information about this person?
   Yes   No

3. Does the writer give specific information?   Yes   No

4. Does the writer use *used to* correctly?   Yes   No

5. Are there any language mistakes? (Please write them here.)
   Yes   No

   _____

   _____

Make corrections to your writing.

PUTTING IT ALL TOGETHER

◆ **Use What You Have Learned**

1. Write about another teenager. If you like, write about yourself as a teenager.

2. If possible, interview two teenagers from the United States or Canada. Ask them what they think about, what they like to do, and what they want to be when they are older. Write their answers. Present the results of your interviews in class.

Test-Taking Tip

Look for the easiest questions on a test and answer these questions first. When you answer the easiest questions first, you will feel more confident about going on to the other questions on the test. Answering these questions first will also help you save time to work on the more difficult questions later in the test.

◆ **Check Your Progress**

On a scale of 1 to 5, rate how well you have mastered the goals set at the beginning of the chapter:

1 2 3 4 5   write a paragraph about a teenager you know.

1 2 3 4 5   learn more parts of speech to write more correct sentences.

1 2 3 4 5   tell the difference between general and specific ideas in sentences.

1 2 3 4 5   learn about cultural differences.

1 2 3 4 5   practice using the past habitual verb tense to write about the past.

If you've given yourself a 3 or lower on any of these goals:

- visit the *Tapestry* web site for additional practice.
- ask your instructor for extra help.
- review the sections of the chapter that you found difficult.
- work with a partner or study group to further your progress.

"The only way to have a friend is to be one."

—Ralph Waldo Emerson

What do you think the quotation means?

Do you agree with Emerson?

In what ways can one "be a friend"?

RECIPE FOR FRIENDSHIP

Everybody has friends. We have old friends, new friends, family friends, and friends of friends. We even have lost friends whom we find again when we are older. Some people enjoy many friends, while others spend time with just one or two special people. There are many ways to be a good friend. In this chapter, you will read and think about making and keeping friends.

Setting Goals

In this chapter you will learn how to:

◈ write about how to make a friendship strong.

In order to do this, you will:

◈ talk before you write in order to use new language and expand your ideas.

◈ practice using your experience as support for your ideas to make your writing stronger.

◈ study in pairs in order to make your studying fun and efficient.

◈ read an advice column and a legend to prepare for writing.

◈ learn to use cause-result expressions.

◇Getting Started   Think about some of your good friends. When did you meet? Why did you become friends? How would you describe your friendship? Jot down some facts about your good friends.

Names of Three Good Friends	When Did You Meet?	Why Did You Become Friends?	Describe Your Friendship
Constance	When we were in high school	We were very similar	Old; we know each other well

MEETING THE TOPIC

LANGUAGE LEARNING STRATEGY

Talk before you write in order to expand your ideas and use new language. When you talk with friends or classmates, you can explain your ideas about a topic and you can practice using new words and expressions. Then, when you put your thoughts into words, you will write more clearly.

Apply the Strategy

Talk with a classmate about friendship. Ask and answer these questions:

- What should a person do to keep a friendship strong?
- How can good friends become "weak" friends?
- Are there friendship differences between men and women? What do you think men want in a friendship? What do women want?

Expanding Your Ideas

Think about the most important "pieces" in a strong friendship, and make a "friendship pie." First, read some "ingredients" that make a friendship pie. Then create your pie by creating "slices." Make big slices for the ingredients that are important in a friendship. Make small slices for the ingredients that are less important in a friendship. You can add or omit any ingredients. When you are finished, show your pie to a classmate.

A friend in need is a friend indeed.

—AMERICAN PROVERB

Some Ingredients for Friendship

Helpfulness: Friends help each other whenever they can.

Loyalty: Friends don't leave their friends.

Honesty: Friends don't lie to their friends. They tell the truth.

Open communication: Friends tell each other personal information.

Frequent communication: Friends see and/or talk to each other often.

Common experiences and/or interests: Friends share past experiences or common interests.

A handful of friends is better than a wagon of gold.

—CZECHOSLOVAKIAN PROVERB

Freewrite

Freewrite about what makes a good friend. Answer any of these questions to begin. Then write some other ideas about friendship.

- What must you do to be a good friend?
- What must you *never* do if you want to build a strong friendship?
- Think of a strong friendship you have. How did it become strong?
- What advice do you have for someone who wants to build a strong friendship?

You will use the ideas from this writing for your assignment later.

Grammar You Can Use: Cause-Result Sentences

Expressions of cause and result are useful when writing about friendship. Learn the following sentence patterns:

_____result_____ **because** _____cause_____.

*I want to be his friend **because** we both like to sing.*
*They went to the coffee shop together **because** they wanted to meet a friend.*
*Honesty makes a friendship strong **because** it builds trust.*

Because _____cause_____, _____result_____.

Because we were in the same class, we began studying together.
Because Juan traveled, he didn't see Josefina for two years.
Because we didn't see each other for several years, our friendship ended.

Practice these patterns by writing three sentences using the causes and results below and two sentences using your own causes and results.

CAUSES	RESULTS
they both like Japanese food	they're close friends
she lies sometimes	they became friends
they met ten years ago	they know a lot about each other
they send e-mail messages every day	they don't trust each other

Do unto others as you would have them do unto you.

—HEBREW PROVERB

1. _____

_____

2. _____
_____

3. _____
_____

4. _____
_____

5. _____
_____

TUNING IN: "Love Doctor"

The video in this chapter is about a man who gives advice about friendships, mostly between men and women. His first book, *Men Are from Mars, Women Are from Venus*, became a best-seller. What advice would you give a man about being friends with a woman? How about a woman who wants to be friends with a man? Watch this video, then answer the questions.

1. What does Gray recommend for improving relationships?

   a. therapy

   b. entertainment

   c. both of these

2. Which sentence is true?

   a. John Gray is a medical doctor.

   b. John Gray has a Ph.D.

   c. Both of these.

3. Gray has sold millions of books. Does everyone agree with Gray's philosophy?

   a. yes

   b. no

4. What does Gray say about all TV sitcoms?

   a. None of them are about relationships between men and women.

   b. All of them are about relationships between men and women.

   c. They are simplistic.

5. What does Gray say is unique about his message?

   a. It's male-friendly.

   b. It's female-friendly.

   c. It's baloney.

LANGUAGE LEARNING STRATEGY

Use your experience as support for your ideas in writing. Good writers develop their ideas through description, explanation, and examples. Examples from the writer's personal experiences can be powerful support. Think about using descriptions of past events to support your ideas in writing.

Apply the Strategy

Support the following ideas by writing about your personal experiences. Begin by reading the example.

Idea: Many women know how to be caring friends.

Your experience as support: I know this statement is true because I have three sisters. They always have lots of special friends. They always do nice things for their friends. They buy their friends gifts. They write their friends letters when they travel. And they listen to their friends when they have problems. I'm a guy, and I have fewer friends than my sisters.

Idea: Friendship is strong when you and your friend have the same interests.

Your experience as support: _____

_____

_____

Idea: It is important to do the same things for your friends as you want them to do for you.

Your experience as support: _____

_____

_____

Idea: It is not always easy to make friends or keep them.

Your experience as support: _____

_____

_____

EXPANDING YOUR LANGUAGE

◇**Vocabulary Check**

The following words and expressions will help you with the reading and writing activities in this chapter. Which ones do you know? Check them off. Look up the definitions of words you don't know and add them to the Vocabulary Section of your Writer's Portfolio.

_____ caring

_____ close friend

_____ conflict

_____ cruel

_____ depend on someone

_____ depend on something

_____ drop someone

_____ feel hurt

_____ follow advice

_____ forgive

_____ give advice

_____ give up

_____ honesty

_____ inseparable

_____ lie

_____ loyalty

_____ make a friend

_____ make a sacrifice (for someone)

Vocabulary Building

1. Match the expressions in Column 1 to the examples in Column 2.

COLUMN 1: EXPRESSIONS	COLUMN 2: EXAMPLES
Andrew **feels hurt.**	They are always together.
Jill and Jennifer are **inseparable.**	They talk almost every day.
John **depends on** Pete and Charlie.	He stayed with his friend instead of going to the concert.
Jackie is **cruel** to her old friend.	He expects his close friends to help him.
Doug and Donna are **close friends.**	She is not kind when she insults her friend.
Ben **made a sacrifice.**	He is sad because his girlfriend **dropped** him.

2. Answer these questions by using the boldface expressions from the Vocabulary Check.

   a. How many **friends have you made** since the beginning of this term?

   _____

   _____

   b. Who **gives you advice?** What **advice did you follow** recently?

   _____

   _____

   c. When did you have a **conflict** with a friend? What was the conflict about?

   _____

   _____

3. You have learned new vocabulary from six chapters about several different topics. This is a good time to review the Vocabulary Section of your Writer's Portfolio. Study the words and expressions you still find difficult. How many new words and expressions have you learned?

   a. 20–40

   b. 40–60

   c. 60+

READING FOR WRITING

You will read two selections about friendship. These selections will help you with your writing in this chapter.

Reading 1 is from a popular advice column in *New Woman* magazine. It is an exchange of letters about a problem with a friend. Read about the problem, then read Harriet Lerner's advice. Before you read, talk to a classmate and answer these questions:

- *Dear Abby* and *Ann Landers* are advice columns. Do you ever read advice columns in newspapers or magazines? Which one(s)?

- Is it a good idea to write a letter to someone when you have a problem?

- How do you solve problems with friends?

> **Birds of a feather flock together.**
>
> **—AMERICAN PROVERB**

Reading 1: Friendship Problem

Dear Harriet:

I have two **close friends,** Jo and Brittany. The three of us are **inseparable.** Recently Jo stopped speaking to Brittany because Brittany **lied** to her. Jo **feels hurt.** It's true that Brittany did a terrible thing, but I don't want to **drop** Brittany. Jo wants me to end my friendship with Brittany. I want Jo to **forgive** Brittany. Now I am fighting with Jo. What can I do?

—Sarah

Dear Sarah:

Try to stay friends with each of them. Stay out of the **conflict** between them. Don't get in the middle. But you don't have to be silent. Friendship **depends on honesty.** If Jo asks you how you can stay friends with Brittany, tell her you don't want to lose her friendship. Tell her also that you want everything to be OK. Tell her you care about them both. Be honest with your friends.

—Harriet

1. What did Brittany do?

   a. She dropped her friend.

   b. She lied to her friend.

   c. She rejected her friend.

2. What is the problem?

   a. Jo wants Brittany to drop Sarah.

   b. Brittany wants Jo to drop Sarah.

   c. Jo wants Sarah to drop Brittany.

3. What advice does Harriet give to Sarah?

   a. Be honest.

   b. Drop Brittany.

   c. Get in the middle.

4. This exercise is called a Problem–Solution Write-Around. Follow these instructions:

   a. Choose a secret name. Don't tell anyone.

   b. Write a short letter about a problem you have with a friend. Begin the letter with *Dear Reader,*

   c. Sign the letter with your secret name. Put the letter on a table in the front of the classroom. All students will do this.

   d. Take another student's letter from the table.

   e. Read the problem and write a solution. Sign your letter *Reader.* Put the letter back on the table.

   f. When all students have finished writing solutions, find your letter. Read it. Is it good advice? Follow these steps again if you want more advice.

Dear Reader,

Here is my problem:

_____

_____

_____

_____

Sincerely,

(Secret Name) _____

Dear (Secret Name) _____,

Here is my suggestion:

_____

_____

_____

_____

Sincerely,

(Reader) _____

Reading 2 is a legend from Greece. A **legend** is an ancient story. This is about two friends and what one did for the other. Before you read, talk to a classmate and answer these questions:

- What would a true friend give up for another in order to prove his or her friendship? Would the friend give up his or her possessions? Job? Family? Life?

- Have you ever made a sacrifice for a friend? What was it?

Reading 2: A Greek Tale of Friendship

Long ago, a **cruel** king lived in Greece. He was cruel to his own people and even crueler to people from other countries. A fine man named Pythias came to this land with his good friend Damon. The cruel king put Pythias in prison. "Pythias must die," said the king. Damon begged the king to change his mind. But the

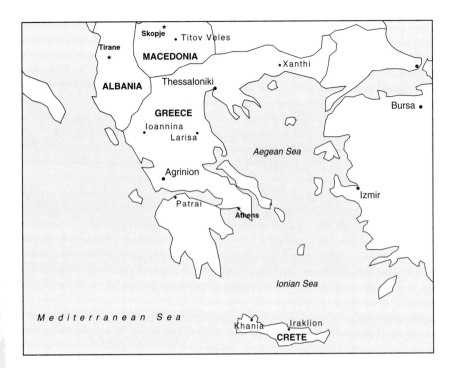

> **What you do not want others to do to you, do not to others.**
>
> **—CONFUCIUS**

king insisted. Pythias asked for one last thing. "I want to see my wife and baby before I die." The king laughed. "No! You will never return." Then Damon offered to go to prison in place of Pythias. "If Pythias does not return," said Damon, "then I will die." The king agreed, but he did not believe that Pythias was going to return. Pythias promised to return. He went home to his country. His wife and friends asked him not to return, but he said he must return. He sadly left for Greece. On the way there was a terrible storm, and he arrived in Greece late. On the last day Damon was prepared to die. "It is better if I die," he said to himself. "I have no wife and baby." Just as Damon was ready to die, Pythias appeared. He ran to take Damon's place. The king ordered "Stop! I have never seen such a strong friendship. You both must live. I hope that some day I can find friends like you two."

1. Put the following sentences from "A Greek Tale of Friendship" in the correct order.

_____ a. Damon offers to stay in prison for Pythias.

_____ b. The king puts Pythias in prison.

_____ c. Damon and Pythias travel to a new country.

_____ d. The king does not kill Damon or Pythias.

_____ e. Pythias returns.

_____ f. Damon and Pythias are close friends.

_____ g. The king promises to kill Pythias.

_____ h. The king says he will kill Damon if Pythias does not return.

_____ i. The king admires their friendship.

_____ j. Pythias wants to see his wife and baby one last time.

2. Damon is a very loyal friend. Imagine you are Damon. What do you say or do in the following cases?

a. Pythias is very ill.

I will search all over the world for the best medicine.

What else? _____

_____

b. Pythias asks you: "What can I do to repay you for your friend-ship?"

What do you say? _____

_____

3. Write a short letter to the king. Tell him how to make a friend.

_____

_____

_____

_____

_____

FROM READING TO WRITING

Getting Ready to Write

Choose a Topic

You are going to write a paragraph about friendship. Explain what contributes to a strong friendship.
You can write about:

- the most important "ingredients" of a strong friendship

- two people you know who have a strong friendship

- two people you know who don't have a strong friendship and what they should do to improve their friendship

- a serious friendship problem you know about and what advice you have in order to solve it

- a strong friendship you have with another person and why it is strong

Choose your topic and write it here:

I will write about _____

_____.

Here are some instructions for writing:

Instructions for Writing About Friendship

1. Begin with the two or three things you consider important in a friendship. Remember that writers often begin with **general** ideas. Here are some examples from this chapter:

   - *Many women know how to be caring friends.*

   - *A strong friendship depends on kindness and common interests.*

2. Describe specific examples that show what you mean. Here are some examples:

   - *They always do nice things for their friends.*

   - *We both play the viola, like sports, and love* Star Trek.

3. When possible, use your experience as support. Read these examples:

   - *I know this because I have three sisters.*

   - *I have a close friendship with someone online.*

Study a Student Example

Before you write, read this paragraph by a high school student.

My AOL Pal

A strong friendship depends on kindness and common interests. I have a close friendship with someone online. We both play the viola, like sports, and love *Star Trek*. Sometimes we organize a *Star Trek* chat room and play *Star Trek* games. We always exchange information about the latest sports games. Sometimes we talk about music. Our friendship is built on

kindness as well as similarities. When I am upset, my online friend encourages me. He makes jokes to cheer me up. I am happy after I send an e-mail message to him. He says he is going to cancel his online account. I suppose I should meet this close friend.

—Anonymous

1. What three common interests do these friends have?

   a. _____

   b. _____

   c. _____

2. What does *upset* mean?

   a. unhappy

   b. kind

   c. cheerful

3. What is one thing you noticed and liked about "My AOL Pal"?

   _____

   _____

4. What is one question or suggestion you have for the author of "My AOL Pal"?

   _____

   _____

Write

Now write your own paragraph using the topic you chose on pages 115–116. Review what you have learned in this chapter. Use the writing you've already done.

After You Write

ACADEMIC POWER STRATEGY

Study in pairs in order to improve your performance in school. Working with another student can help you do well in school. You can clarify questions, increase your vocabulary, and practice your skills. It is often easier to remember material you learn with a classmate. It is also very helpful to work with a partner when revising your writing. Another classmate can point out confusing ideas or mistakes in your writing that you don't see. Study in pairs for all your classes and whenever you revise your writing.

Apply the Strategy

Revise

First, have someone look at the ideas in your writing. Give your finished paragraph to a classmate. Your classmate will complete these statements.

1. The writing is about these ingredients of a strong friendship:

_____

2. These are specific examples that show what the writer means:

a. _____

b. _____

Can the writer add more examples? Where?

_____

_____

3. The writer uses this experience as support:

_____

_____

4. The writer can add or change this to improve the paragraph:

_____

_____

Make changes to improve your writing.

Edit

Now have someone check your writing for organization and language. Give your revised paragraph to a classmate. Your classmate will answer these questions.

1. Does the writer begin with some general ideas about friendship?
   Yes   No

2. Does the writer give specific examples?   Yes   No

   If the answer is no, where can the writer add some specific examples?

   _____

3. Does the writer use cause-result expressions correctly?
   Yes   No

   If the answer is no, which words should be corrected?

   _____

(continued on next page)

4. Are there any language mistakes? (Please write them here.)
Yes   No

_____

Make corrections to your writing.

PUTTING IT ALL TOGETHER

Use What You Have Learned

1. There are lots of movies about friends. Choose a movie that interests you and write about it. Share your writing with the class.

2. Ask two friends outside of class what their recipe for friendship is. Present the interview results to your class.

Test-Taking Tip

Make sure you understand all the directions on the test before you begin. Read the instructions slowly and carefully. If there is anything you are confused about, ask your teacher to explain. Don't be shy about asking for more information. There will probably be other students who are confused about the same thing you are asking about.

CHECK YOUR PROGRESS

On a scale of 1 to 5, rate how well you have mastered the goals set at the beginning of the chapter:

1 2 3 4 5   write about how to make a friendship strong.

1 2 3 4 5   talk before you write in order to use new language and expand your ideas.

1 2 3 4 5   use your experience as support for your ideas to make your writing stronger.

1 2 3 4 5   study in pairs in order to make your studying fun and efficient.

1 2 3 4 5   use cause-result expressions.

If you've given yourself a 3 or lower on any of these goals:

- visit the *Tapestry* web site for additional practice.
- ask your instructor for extra help.
- review the sections of the chapter that you found difficult.
- work with a partner or study group to further your progress.

"Before all else, we are daughters or sons. Our relationships with our parents are the most influential in our lives, and they are never simple."

—Harriet Lerner

How many generations are represented in the photo?

How important are parents in the lives of their children?

Do you agree with the quotation?

7

MAMAS
AND PAPAS

In this chapter you'll read about people and their parents. What do you appreciate most about your parents? Are there people in your life who act like parents? Perhaps they are good friends, aunts and uncles, or grandparents. You'll read and think about the role of parents, then you'll write a portrait.

Setting Goals

In this chapter you will learn how to:

◈ write about your mother or father, or someone who acted like a parent to you.

In order to do this, you will:

◈ learn to make and use an "Idea File" to increase your creativity and store ideas for writing.

◈ learn how to show what you mean by using specific details when you write.

◈ learn to manage your time carefully as a writing student.

◈ read two selections about parents in order to prepare for writing.

◈ learn to use pronouns correctly.

◇ **Getting Started**

Think about your parents or a person in your life who acted like a parent: a family friend, an aunt, an uncle, or a grandparent. Think about where they are, what they do, and how you feel about them. Jot down some words and expressions about this person.

_____

_____

_____

_____

MEETING THE TOPIC

◇ **Talk with a Partner**

Look at these photos of parents and children. Talk about where they come from and how they are related. Then, "introduce" the person you wrote about in Getting Started. Do you have a photograph of this person? Bring it to class. Try to get to know your partner's parent better, too. Ask and answer these questions. Add more information.

- Where was your parent born, and where does your parent live now?
- What language does your parent speak?
- Is your parent traditional or modern?
- What important memory do you have about your parent?
- What do you want to do for your parent?
- What do you want to say to your parent?
- Are parent–child relationships different across cultures?

LANGUAGE LEARNING STRATEGY

Keep an "Idea File" to increase your creativity and store ideas for writing. There are many times when thoughts come to mind and you don't have time to think or read or write about them. When this happens, jot down the new idea in an Idea File so that you can refer to it later. This way, you will always have interesting topics for your journal and future writing assignments.

Apply the Strategy

Create a new section in your Writer's Portfolio. Call it your Idea File, and add enough pages to record new ideas whenever they occur. Begin by jotting down some ideas you have now. These could be ideas for future writing topics or stories from your past that you would like to tell. Add new ideas to your Idea File regularly.

◇ Freewrite

Freewrite about your mother or father. Answer any of these questions to begin. Then write some other things about your parent.

- Which parent are you writing about?
- What comes to mind when you think of this person?
- What are some special memories you have about this person?
- Describe an event that happened with this person.
- How does this person feel about you?
- How do you feel about this person?

Freewriting helps you improve your writing fluency. If you freewrite regularly, you increase your speed and writing becomes easier. You also get ideas on paper to be used as the "seeds" of later writing assignments.

TUNING IN: "Letting Go"

This video is about parents "letting go" of their children. You will watch families say good-bye to their children as they begin college. It is a "bittersweet" experience for all, as the reporter says. Read the questions, watch the video, and then answer the questions. Watch the video several times to check your answers.

1. Emily's parents help her get settled at Washington University. What do they say?

   a. "We have driven from Atlanta."

   b. "There is plenty of space in Emily's room."

   c. "This is the happiest and saddest experience."

2. Emily's parents believe that they have to "let go." What does this mean?

   a. They have to talk to Emily on the phone every day.

   b. They have to let their child grow into an adult.

   c. They have to pay all the bills.

3. At Emily's university, there is an orientation for

   a. nervous freshmen.

   b. anxious parents.

   c. both of these.

4. An expert says that parents must

   a. acknowledge the changes that are taking place in their children.

   b. support and enjoy the changes.

   c. both of these.

5. Letting go of children is

   a. expensive.

   b. confusing.

   c. boring.

© CNN

We never know the love of a parent until we become parents ourselves.

—HENRY WARD BEECHER

EXPANDING YOUR LANGUAGE

Vocabulary Check

These words and expressions will help you with the reading and writing in this chapter. Check those that you know. Learn the definitions of new words and add them to the Vocabulary Section of your Writer's Portfolio.

_____ be devoted to   _____ nightmare

_____ be surrounded by   _____ refer to

_____ call upon   _____ replace

_____ come to mind   _____ start a new life

_____ fierce   _____ struggle

_____ luxury

Review the following words from previous chapters. You will find them useful in writing about mothers and fathers:

forgive	immigrant
be determined	hard-working
be unafraid	have an effect on
have a dream	make someone feel (happy, sad, etc.)

Vocabulary Building

1. On the next page, match the words or expressions in Column 1 to those with the same meaning in Column 2.

COLUMN 1	COLUMN 2
fierce	fight
be surrounded	bad dream
struggle	enter one's thoughts
replace	take the place of
call upon	excuse
forgive	strong
nightmare	be in the center
come to mind	reach for

2. Answer these questions with words from the Vocabulary Check.

   a. Write about a movie star who lives in **luxury.** Where does this person live? What does she or he buy? Write about how this person lives.

   _____

   _____

   _____

   _____

   b. Write about a person you know who **is devoted to** someone or something. Describe what this person does to show how she or he is devoted.

   _____

   _____

   _____

   _____

   c. Write about a time in your life when you had to **struggle.** Describe where you were, what you did, what you wanted to achieve, and how you felt.

   _____

   _____

   _____

   _____

Grammar You Can Use: Personal Pronouns

A **pronoun** is a word that is used in place of a noun. You will want to include pronouns in your writing to reduce repetition and make your writing smooth. Review these rules:

- All pronouns replace or refer to nouns.

- Singular pronouns: *I, you, he, she, it*

- Plural pronouns: *we, you, they* (Notice that *you* can be singular or plural.)

- Pronouns can be **subjects** or **objects**. They are called **subject pronouns** *or* **object pronouns**. Subjects *cause* the action of the verb, and objects *receive* the action of the verb.

Read the examples of personal pronouns in the chart.

PERSONAL PRONOUNS			
Singular			
	Subject	**Object**	**Examples**
			Family Reunion
First Person	I	me	**I** talk to Aunt Julie every week. She helps **me** plan our annual family reunion.
Second Person	you	you	Aunt Julie says, "**You** miss Grandpa. And he misses **you**."
Third Person	he, she, it	him, her, it	That's why **she** organizes the reunion. I am so grateful to **her**.

Plural			
First Person	we	us	**We** get together every year. The reunion keeps **us** in touch.
Second Person	you	you	**You** can all join us this year. We want to include all of **you**.
Third Person	they	them	All of my family members will be there. **They** want to meet you. You'll like **them**!

Use the paragraph frame from "Family Reunion" to practice using personal pronouns. Write about people and events in your family. Change words and sentences to make the sentences true for you. Be careful to use the correct form of the verb.

(Pronoun) ＿＿＿＿＿＿＿＿ talk to (name) ＿＿＿＿＿＿＿＿

every (measure of time) ＿＿＿＿＿＿＿＿. (Pronoun)

＿＿＿＿＿＿＿＿ helps (pronoun) ＿＿＿＿＿＿＿＿

(action) ＿＿＿＿＿＿＿＿. (Name) ＿＿＿＿＿＿＿＿ says,

"(Pronoun) ＿＿＿＿＿＿＿＿ (action) ＿＿＿＿＿＿＿＿

(Name) ＿＿＿＿＿＿＿＿. And (pronoun) ＿＿＿＿＿＿＿＿

(action) ＿＿＿＿＿＿＿＿ (pronoun) ＿＿＿＿＿＿＿＿." That's

why (pronoun) ＿＿＿＿＿＿＿＿ (action) ＿＿＿＿＿＿＿＿.

(Pronoun) ＿＿＿＿＿＿＿＿ feel/s so (feeling) ＿＿＿＿＿＿＿＿

to (pronoun) ＿＿＿＿＿＿＿＿.

ACADEMIC POWER STRATEGY

Learn to manage your time carefully as a writing student. Writing is a difficult skill for all students: native speakers and second language learners. Learning to write takes time. If you manage your time well, you will be able to write more and better. The best way to learn to write is to write a lot. Read these tips for managing your time.

Tips for Time Management

1. **Set goals.** Students who have a vision of their future are usually successful. Set a new goal for each writing assignment. Make sure that your goal is realistic.

2. **Make a timeline for each writing assignment.** Include all the tasks you want to do. Set dates for each task. Stick to your schedule.

3. **For every one hour in class, study for two hours.** Writing takes time. Give yourself time to improve your skills.

Apply the Strategy

Follow the **Tips for Time Management** in this exercise.

1. What is one goal for your writing in this chapter? What would you like to learn or improve?

   _____

2. Write the dates for these tasks:

TASK	DATE
I will complete the exercises in this chapter.	_____
I will read and understand the reading selections in this chapter.	_____
I will choose a writing topic.	_____
I will write a first draft.	_____
I will revise my first draft.	_____
I will edit my writing.	_____
I will give my final draft to the teacher or put it in my portfolio.	_____

READING FOR WRITING

In this chapter, you will read two selections about parents. Pay attention to the language and ideas. These readings will help you with your writing in this chapter.

Reading 1 is by a writer who has mixed feelings about his father. Children can have both negative and positive feelings about their parents. Children remember both the good times and the bad times. Talk to a classmate and answer the following questions before you read:

- Does anyone in your family have mixed feelings about another family member?

- Think about a time when you forgave another person. Is forgiving another person easy or difficult?

Reading 1: Forgiving Dad

> If we can learn to view our parents more calmly and objectively, then our other relationships will be easy.
>
> —HARRIET LERNER

When I was seven, my father told me that I was too big to hug him good-night.[1] Ever since that evening, I haven't really liked him very much. Throughout my early years, Dad was distant, sad, troubled. He couldn't manage his marriage or his responsibilities as a father. Through my early adolescence, Dad didn't come home every night and he spent money carelessly. My mother, brother, and I tried to protect my father. We told stories to curious friends and family members that hid the truth. But my mother was hurt and lonely and my brother and I began to feel angry. I decided never to forgive my father for hurting my mother and for making my childhood sad.

For the last twelve years, Dad and I have kept our distance. We see each other regularly, but we don't move beyond pleasant conversation. This year, however, my sometimes funny, entertaining father has been warm and charming. I find myself encouraged and confused when I am with him. I'm happy that some day I may change the decision I made twelve years ago. I also know that forgiveness takes a long, long time.

—Lars Anderson

[1]to hug someone goodnight: to embrace someone before going to bed.

1. Why does the writer say that he doesn't like his father very much?

   a. His father is sometimes funny and entertaining.

   b. His father was distant.

   c. His father knows that forgiveness takes a long time.

2. What did the writer and his brother do to protect their father?

   a. They told stories to hide the truth.

   b. They spent money carelessly.

   c. They didn't hug him goodnight.

3. Use the paragraph frame from "Forgiving Dad" to write about something a parent said to you as a child that taught you something important. Add, omit, or change words to make the writing true for you.

> **How many hopes and fears, how many ardent wishes and anxious apprehensions are twisted together in the threads that connect the parent with the child.**
>
> **—SAMUEL GRISWOLD GOODRICH**

   When I was (age) _____, my (mother or father) _____ told me _____.
   Ever since then, _____.
   Through my early adolescence, _____. I decided _____. For the last few years, _____. This year I find myself _____. I know that _____.

Reading 2 is a selection about the writer's mother. Before you read, answer these questions with a classmate:

• What do most parents want for their children?

• Why do people leave their native countries?

• Have your parents moved to a new city, country, or continent?

Reading 2: My Mother in the Land of the Golden Mountain

Her trip to America from her war-torn country was a **nightmare.** She rode a bicycle from dawn to darkness for days. She fought **fierce** winds from all directions and crashing waves on a small ship in the open sea. She walked miles and miles until her feet were full of pain. My mother **struggled** hard to find a life of freedom and happiness. She finally found it here in the land of the "Golden Mountain." In 1981, my mother **started a new life.** She was very poor at the beginning. She worked day and night and finally had enough money to work at only one job.

My mother taught me the greatest lesson of a lifetime. She taught me that people can succeed if they try as hard as they can and if they **call upon** the power within themselves. If people don't try, happiness will not come to them. Today my mother has finally arrived at a place of **luxury** and freedom. She **is surrounded by** her loving family in the land of the "Golden Mountain" with a life filled with golden moments.

—Victor Ly

1. Put these sentences in the right order. Change the verb tenses so that they are correct. (Refer to Chapter 1 to review present and past tense.)

_____ a. Victor's mother has more than one job.

_____ b. Victor's mother is happy.

_____ c. Victor's mother teaches him an important lesson.

_____ d. Victor's mother has a difficult time leaving her country.

_____ e. Victor's mother arrives in a new country.

2. What is the main idea that the writer is trying to show about his mother?

   a. She struggled and never gave up.

   b. She waited for happiness to come to her.

   c. She had three children.

3. What lesson about success did Victor learn from his mother?

   a. Success comes from good luck.

   b. Success comes if you move to the land of the "Golden Mountain."

   c. Success comes from hard work.

4. If you have children one day, what important lesson do you want to teach them?

   _____

   _____

main Idea

LANGUAGE LEARNING STRATEGY

"**S**how" what you mean by using specific details when you write. Good writers use specific details to help the reader "see" and "experience" what they are describing. You studied strong adjectives in Chapter 4. Another way to develop specific details is to expand "telling" sentences into "showing" descriptions. Telling sentences do not give the reader a "picture" or "experience." Showing descriptions add the details that make the writing "come alive." Showing writing helps the reader imagine that he or she is actually experiencing something, not reading about it. Look at the following example:

(continued on next page)

Telling sentence: *My grandmother teaches me about my culture.*

Showing description: *She comes from China and speaks Chinese to me even when I answer in English. She loves to play Mah-jongg with her friends. When she can't play with her friends, she plays with me. She taught me how to make dumplings for Chinese New Year. And I can even write Chinese calligraphy. Thanks to my grandmother, I am proud of my heritage.*

Apply the Strategy

Develop one of the telling sentences into a description that shows what you mean.

1. I admire all of my relatives, but the person I admire most is my grandfather (mother, uncle, etc.).

2. My mom (grandfather, uncle, cousin, etc.) is very kind to people.

3. (S)he struggled very hard.

4. We had an important conversation.

_____

_____

_____

_____

FROM READING TO WRITING

Getting Ready to Write

Choose a Topic

You are going to write about your mother or father or someone who acted like a parent when you were younger. Choose one of the following topics:

- Write about a parent you admire.

- Write about a parent you have grown to appreciate.

- Write about something important you learned from a parent, either through observation or by direct teaching.

Choose your topic and write it here:

I will write about _____.

Here are some instructions for writing:

Instructions for Writing About a Parent

1. Begin your paper in an interesting way. Introduce your mother or father so that the reader wants to continue reading. Here are some examples of introductions in this chapter:

   - *When I was seven, my father told me that I was too big to hug him good-night.*

   - *Her trip to America from her war-torn country was a nightmare.*

2. Choose one main idea to develop about your mother or father. Don't write everything you know or remember. Here are examples of main ideas from the readings in this chapter:

   - *Although my father was distant when I was young, I am beginning to forgive him.*

   - *My mother struggled hard to achieve success.*

   - *My father is a talented man.*

3. Support the main idea of your writing by "showing" what you want the reader to see or feel. Use specific details. Look at this example:

   - *She rode a bicycle from dawn to darkness for days. She fought fierce winds from all directions and crashing waves on a small ship in the open sea. She walked miles and miles until her feet were full of pain.*

Study a Student Example

Read the student example, which is a model for the writing you will do in this chapter.

My Dad

Bang! Bang! Bang! That's the sound of a hammer on the wood of my bird house. And there, it is finished! My dad and I just finished making a masterpiece. Hi! I'm Barry Young. Do you have someone in your life that is so great you can't stop thinking about him? Well, I do and his name is Ying Young and he is my dad.

My dad is very talented. He used to be a master cook. And he is a good electrician. But his best achievement (in my opinion) is that he's an expert in wood. He is a true craftsman and he can make anything he

> **The hand that rocks the cradle is the hand that rules the world.**
>
> —W. S. ROSS

thinks of. Most of the furniture in our house is my dad's work. He makes shelves, desks, tables, and chairs. You name it—he makes it. When my dad starts projects, I watch him. "Some day you will be just like me," he says, "creative and skilled." (He speaks to me in Cantonese.) I like it when he says that because it gives me a goal—something to reach for. I like working with wood too. But I make small things, fun things instead of useful things. Someday I'll make useful things like my dad. And maybe I'll learn to cook like him too.

—Barry Young

Answer these questions:

1. The writer includes sounds in "My Dad." Write down two things you "hear" in this selection.

   a. _____

   b. _____

2. The writer presents one main idea about his dad. Which is the main idea?

   a. My dad is kind and helpful.

   b. My dad used to be a master cook.

   c. My dad is an expert in wood.

3. What is one thing you noticed and liked about the writing?

   _____

   _____

   _____

   _____

4. What is one question or suggestion you have?

   _____

   _____

   _____

   _____

Write

Now write about the topic you chose on page 136. Review what you have learned in this chapter. Use the writing you've already begun.

After You Write

Revise

First, have someone look at the **ideas** in your writing. Give your finished paragraph to a classmate. Your classmate will complete these statements:

1. The writing is about this person:

   _____

2. The writer develops this main idea about his or her parent:

   _____

   _____

3. The writer helps the reader "see" and "experience" the writing through these showing descriptions:

   _____

   _____

   _____

4. The writer could add or change this to improve the paragraph:

   _____

   _____

   _____

Make changes to improve your writing.

Edit

Now have someone check your writing for **organization and language**. Give your revised paragraph to a classmate. Your classmate will answer these questions:

1. Does the writer begin the piece and introduce the person in an interesting way that makes the reader want to continue?
   Yes   No

2. Does the writer use **pronouns** correctly?   Yes   No

   If the answer is no, which words should be corrected?

   _____

   _____

3. Are there any language mistakes? (Please write them here.)
Yes   No

_____

_____

_____

Make corrections to your writing.

PUTTING IT ALL TOGETHER

1. Write about another parent or someone who acted like a parent when you were younger. Perhaps this is a grandparent or an older sister or brother. Try to make your writing interesting and correct.

2. Watch a movie about relationships across generations. Write about the relationship in the movie. Talk about it with your classmates.

Test-Taking Tip

Underline key words on an essay test before you begin writing your essay. Make sure you understand what you are being asked to do before you start writing. For example, if you are being asked to compare two things, make sure your essay shows how the two things are similar. If you are asked to describe something, make sure you explain the thing you are writing about as clearly and in as much detail as you can. If you are asked to summarize something, make sure you give a short statement of the main points or facts.

CHECK YOUR PROGRESS

On a scale of 1 to 5, rate how well you have mastered the goals set at the beginning of the chapter:

1 2 3 4 5   write about your mother or father, or someone who acted like a parent.

1 2 3 4 5   make and use an "Idea File" to increase your creativity and store ideas for writing.

1 2 3 4 5   show what you mean by using specific details when you write.

1 2 3 4 5   learn to manage your time carefully as a writing student.

1 2 3 4 5   learn to use pronouns correctly.

If you've given yourself a 3 or lower on any of these goals:

- visit the *Tapestry* web site for additional practice.
- ask your instructor for extra help.
- review the sections of the chapter that you found difficult.
- work with a partner or study group to further your progress.

"No big technology in history has taken off more swiftly, more breathtakingly, than the car. And nowhere did it take off faster than in America."

—Bill Bryson

How does the person in the photo feel about his car?

What does the quotation mean?

Do you think cars are important in North America? Why?

8

FINDING YOUR WAY

This chapter is about cars and driving. Not everyone drives a car in Canada or the United States, but almost everyone rides in cars. Because cars and driving are such an important part of life in the twenty-first century, it is important to know about them. After doing some language exercises and reading and thinking, you will write about cars and driving.

Setting Goals

In this chapter you will learn how to:

◈ write instructions about how to drive or buy a car.

In order to do this, you will:

◈ use diagrams to help you plan and organize your writing.

◈ learn to anticipate reader questions in order to include important information in your writing.

◈ read two selections about cars and driving to get ready to write.

◈ use a computer when you write.

◈ learn expressions of obligation.

◆ Getting Started

Write a timeline of important events in your life related to cars and driving. Write the year above the timeline. Below the timeline, write the event. Begin with these events and add more:

rode in a car for the first time	bought a car
learned to drive	sold a car
got my driver's license	changed a tire

EXAMPLE:

Year:	1983		1997	1998	1999
Event:	Rode in a car for the first time		Got my permit	Drove for the first time	Got my license

A Personal Timeline of My History with Cars

Year:

_____

Event:

> In 1898, there were fewer than thirty cars in the United States. In 1915, there were two million cars. In 1920, there were ten million.

MEETING THE TOPIC

◆ Talk with a Partner

Discuss the photos. Jot down as much information as you can for each of the cars. Write:

- which country they come from
- when they were popular
- what they are/were good for
- your opinion of this car

a. _____

_____

_____

_____

b. _____

_____

_____

_____

c. _____

_____

_____

_____

d. _____

e. _____

f. _____

 Freewrite

Now freewrite about a car that interests you in some way. Answer any of these questions to begin:

- What does the car look like?
- Where is the car made?
- What interests you about the car?

- Can you drive this car?
- What else do you know about this car?

The purpose of the freewrite is to get your early ideas on paper. You will expand this writing through exercises. You may use part or all of the freewrite for the writing assignment at the end of the chapter.

TUNING IN:
"Tough Teen Driving Laws"

This video talks about strict driving laws for teenagers trying to get their driver's license. Watch and listen for where this is filmed and who is affected by the new laws. Then answer the questions.

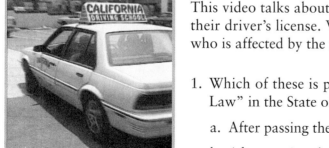

© CNN

1. Which of these is part of the new "Graduated Driver Licensing Law" in the State of California?

   a. After passing the written test, teens cannot drive for 6 months.

   b. After passing the written test, teens cannot get their driver's license for 6 months until they prove they've had 50 hours of driving time with an adult.

   c. After passing the wirtten test, teens can begin to drive immediately.

2. What other statement below is true about the new law?

    a. Teens cannot drive after dark.

    b. An adult must be in the car if a teen is driving after dark.

    c. Teens cannot drive between 12:00 am and 5:00 a.m.

3. What do teens think is the most difficult part of the new law?

    a. Teens are prohibited from having passengers under the age of 20 unless someone over 25 is in the car.

    b. Teens cannot drive after dark.

    c. Teens must prove they have had driving time with an adult before receiving their license.

4. Do all teens think these driving laws are too tough?

    a. yes

    b. no

5. Which state has the "toughest licensing restrictions in the country"?

    a. California

    b. New York

    c. Florida

EXPANDING YOUR LANGUAGE

◇**Vocabulary Check**

These words and expressions will help you write about cars and driving. They will also be helpful when you get to the Reading for Writing section in this chapter. Check the words you already know. Look up the definitions of new words and add them to the Vocabulary Section of your Writer's Portfolio.

_____ break down	_____ point out
_____ commuter	_____ reliable
_____ in good condition	_____ safety
_____ intersection	_____ take a test
_____ motorist	_____ traffic
_____ operate	_____ vehicle

Vocabulary Building

In 1905, a Cadillac was driven up the steps of the Capitol in Washington, D.C., to prove the car's power.

1. Match the words and expressions in Column 1 to words with the **same** meaning in Column 2.

COLUMN 1	COLUMN 2
vehicle	drive
reliable	car or truck
operate	show
point out	driver
motorist	dependable

2. Complete the paragraph. Choose words and expressions from this list.

safe	operate	take care of	in good condition
traffic	intersection	break down	insurance reliable

Nowadays, I really want to have a new car. My 1970 Cadillac is too old, and it is not (a) _____. I bought the car last May, and it seemed (b) _____ and (c) _____. But three months later, I was driving in lots of (d) _____. The car began to make noise. I was sure it was going to (e) _____. The car stopped right in an (f) _____. Now I can't (g) _____ the car. I need a mechanic. I don't know how to (h) _____ car problems. I don't have enough money. I have to pay for (i) _____ and repairs. I really want a new car.

3. Write a short letter to the owner of the Cadillac. Give him advice. Use new words and expressions from this and previous chapters.

Dear Cadillac Owner,

_____

_____

_____

_____

Sincerely,

_____

Grammar You Can Use: Expressions of Obligation

When you write instructions, you tell the reader what to do. The following verbs and **helping** verbs (**auxiliary** verbs) communicate obligation: *must, have to, should, need*. Use these verbs when you write instructions.

- **Must**

  *Every driver **must** be able to start, steer, stop, back up, turn, and park a car.*

- **Have to**

  *A driver does not **have to** be an expert mechanic, but a driver should know when his or her car needs repairs.*

- **Should**

  *Drivers **should** know the basic rules of the road.*

- **Need**

  *A beginning driver **needs** a good teacher.*

Must and *should* are followed by the simple verb. You need to conjugate (give the correct form of) *have to* and *need*. Then:

- *Have to* is followed by a simple verb.
- *Need* is followed by a verb or noun.

Practice using expressions of obligation by answering these questions:

1. What is one thing drivers **should** know if they want to drive in your native country?

_____

2. Do students **need** permits to park on campus? What do they **have to** do to get them?

   _____

   _____

3. What **must** drivers do if they have an accident?

   _____

   _____

READING FOR WRITING

In 1998 there were 20 million licensed drivers in the state of California.

In this chapter you will read two selections about cars and driving. Look for language, organization, and ideas to help you with the writing assignment.

Reading 1 is from a booklet on driving safely. Before you read, talk to a classmate and answer these questions:

- What is the best way to learn to drive?

- What must a driver never do?

Reading 1: How to Drive a Car Safely

Driving is one of the most important skills a person can learn. Driving is fun and convenient, but it is also dangerous. Drivers can do several things to be safe. First, they must learn how to operate a car. This takes training and practice. Second, drivers must learn the rules of the road. They should understand roadway signs and study **traffic** laws. Finally, drivers can avoid accidents when they make decisions to be safe. They should not drive too fast. They should not drive if they are tired. When people follow these instructions, they are safe and responsible drivers.

1. Which of the following are **not** examples of "rules of the road":

    a. Drive in the right-hand lane in Canada and the United States.

    b. A beginning driver needs a good teacher.

    c. The speedometer tells how fast the car is going.

    d. Never drive past a stop sign without stopping.

    e. Always let pedestrians have the right of way.

2. According to the reading selection, what do you think are two common causes of accidents?

    a. People drive too fast for the road conditions.

    b. People do not pass a vision test.

    c. Drivers do not check their tires.

    d. Drivers fall asleep when they are driving.

    e. Drivers talk on the phone when they are driving.

3. Write a short letter to someone you know who is learning to drive. Tell this person what he or she can do to be a safe and careful driver.

    Dear _____,

    _____

    _____

    _____

    _____

    _____

    _____

    _____

    Sincerely,

    _____

Use diagrams to help you plan and organize your writing. In Chapter 1 you learned how graphic organizers can help you organize ideas. You used a **cluster** to write about different kinds of success. A **diagram** is also a graphic organizer. There are several kinds of diagrams. Here are three that are useful for writing instructions:

A **linear diagram** shows the relationship between general and specific ideas. The most general ideas are on the left side. The most specific ideas are on the right side. Here is an example of the linear diagram the writer used to plan "How to Drive a Car Safely."

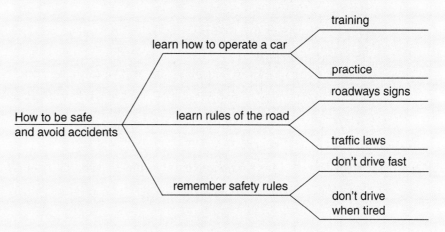

A **flow chart** or a **sequence chain** shows ideas in a specific order.

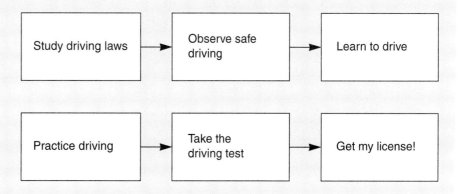

(continued on next page)

A **Venn diagram** shows similarities and differences. (You used a Venn diagram in Chapter 5 on page 94.)

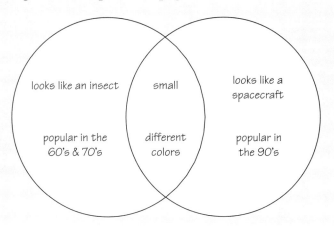

Volkswagen Beetle   Volkswagen UFO

When planning and organizing ideas, you can write words, expressions, or phrases in graphic organizers. You can even include small drawings. (You usually don't write sentences.) Use diagrams to help you plan your writing.

Apply the Strategy

Practice using a diagram by choosing one of these activities:

- Think about two kinds of cars. Use a Venn diagram to write down the similarities and differences between these cars.
- Tell a classmate how to get to the Motor Vehicle Office in your community. Use a flow chart.
- Explain to a friend how to prepare for a driver's test. Use a linear diagram.

Present your diagram to the class.

Reading 2 explains how to get a driver's license. Before you read, talk to a classmate and answer these questions:

- Do you have a driver's license? Did you have to get a permit first?
- What is the most difficult thing about driving?
- Are driving rules in the United States and Canada similar to those in your native culture?

Reading 2: The Driving Test

The driving test is your opportunity to show that you can drive safely. Only you and the examiner can be in the car. Before you take the driving test, you must **take the written and vision tests.** The written tests are available in many languages, but all drivers must show that they can read and understand simple English. When you take the driving test, bring your old license or permit. Bring a car that is safe to drive. The car should be **in good working condition.** You will take the driving test in your car. The examiner will ask you to **point out** the basic controls of the car. Show him or her the headlights, windshield wipers, emergency lights, and the parking brake. You must also show that you have car insurance. Buckle your seat belt before you begin driving. The examiner will ask you to show the arm signals. When you drive, the examiner will observe how you park, turn, steer, drive through traffic, obey the signs, back up, and stop. At the end of the test, the examiner will give you your score sheet and discuss the results with you. If you pass all the tests, you can drive home. Congratulations!

1. Reread "The Driving Test." Underline all the expressions of obligation.

2. What are two things a person must do to before the driving test?

   a. _____

   b. _____

3. What are three things a person must do during the driving test?

   a. _____

   b. _____

   c. _____

LANGUAGE LEARNING STRATEGY

Learn to **anticipate readers' questions** in order to include important information in your writing. When writers anticipate readers' questions, they think about what the readers will want to know. Then writers include this information in their writing. When you do this, you don't omit any important details. Here are some questions the writer of "The Driving Test" thought about before writing:

- How many tests must people take in order to get a driver's license?

- Are the written tests in English only?

- What should people bring to the driving test?

- What does the examiner want to know?

It is a good idea to jot down some possible reader questions before you write. In this way, your writing will be complete.

Apply the Strategy

Use the paragraph frame from "The Driving Test" to write about another process. Choose a process related to cars and driving (washing a car, filling a car with gas, taking the written test, etc.) or another process (cooking something, using a household appliance, opening a bank account, etc.). Add or omit words in the following frame. Before you begin, write three questions that a reader will probably have about the process. Be sure your paragraph answers these questions.

Reader Question 1: _____

Reader Question 2: _____

Reader Question 3: _____

The (name of process) 1. _____ is (explanation of process) 2. _____. Before you (do the process) 3. _____, you must (first requirement) 4. _____. (Explanation of first requirement) 5. _____

_____.

When you (do the process) 6. _____, bring (what to bring or buy) 7. _____. The (required materials) 8. _____ should be (required condition of materials) 9. _____. First, you (first step of the process) 10. _____. Next, you (second step of the process) 11. _____. Finally, you (last step of the process) 12. _____. You must also (one more thing) 13. _____. After the (process) 14. _____, you (what you will do or how you will feel) 15. _____.

FROM READING TO WRITING

◆ Getting Ready to Write

Choose a Topic

Write about cars or driving. Choose a topic from the list below:

1. Write instructions.

   - Explain how to get your driver's permit or driver's license.
   - Teach someone how to drive.
   - Instruct the reader on how to buy a car.
   - Give instructions on how to wash a car (inside and out).

2. Tell a story about an experience related to cars and driving.

   - Write about a time when you were a driver.
   - Write about a time when you were a pedestrian or a passenger.

Choose your topic and write it here:

I will write about _____

_____

Here are some instructions for writing:

Instructions for Writing About Cars and Driving

1. Begin with a sentence that tells why it is important to read your writing. Some examples from this chapter are on the next page:

- *Driving is fun and convenient, but it is also dangerous.*
- *The driving test is your opportunity to show that you can drive safely.*

2. Give a general overview of what you will explain or teach. Here's an example:

- *Drivers can do several things to be safe.*

3. Describe three to five specific ideas. These will be steps, points, or events. Read this example:

- *First, they must learn how to operate a car. Second, drivers must learn the rules of the road. Finally, drivers can avoid accidents when they make decisions to be safe.*

4. Conclude with how your writing helps the reader. Here's an example:

- *When people follow these instructions, they are safe and responsible drivers.*

Study Two Student Examples

In this chapter, you have several choices for writing. This time, there are two student examples to read before you write. The first student example compares Japanese cars and the BMW. The second student example describes one student's early driving experience.

On Japanese Cars

There is a serious problem with Japanese cars. What do you think of Japanese cars? Can you tell the difference between Japanese cars and other cars? I hear often that Japanese cars are **reliable.** But that is all I hear. Japanese car makers don't do enough. In short, the problem is that

Japanese cars don't give the customers "their own world." This means that the customers can't visualize "Japanese life" sitting on the seats of Japanese cars. When I buy a BMW, I buy it because I can see "German life" easily when I am in the car. I can imagine driving on the roads of Europe. I doubt that drivers want to imagine themselves on the roads in Japan. Japanese car makers must work to create a "world" for their customers. They will not succeed in the world's car market.

—Hiroyuki Matsumaru

1. What is the "serious problem" with Japanese cars?

    a. They are not reliable.

    b. The drivers can't visualize another world while in their cars.

    c. They don't drive well on the roads of Europe.

2. What is one thing you noticed and liked about the writing?

    _____

    _____

3. What is one question or suggestion you have?

    _____

    _____

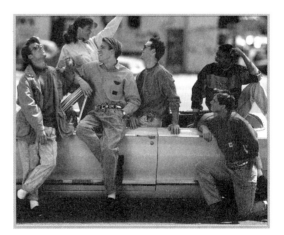

My Early Driving Experience

I did not have a happy birthday when I turned sixteen. My father did not sign my driver's permit application. He said I was too young to drive. I tried to change his mind. I promised not to drive fast. I promised to listen to him. He finally agreed. I was so happy. I got my driver's permit and knew my life was going to improve. I was wrong. First, all my friends asked me to drive them home from school. I had no time. Second, it was

> **Cars have given us motion but taken away dignity. If they have given us freedom, they have also become small prisons.**
>
> **—MARYA MANNES**

so expensive. I bought gas and paid for insurance. I had no money. Finally, I had a car accident. My car had mechanical problems and I was a careless driver. Now I had no car and no confidence. It is a mistake to allow teenagers to drive. My father was right.

—Tzu-Hao Lu

1. What three things happened to change Tzu-Hao's mind about driving at 16?

   a. _____

   b. _____

   c. _____

2. What is one thing you noticed and liked about the writing?

   _____

   _____

   _____

3. What is one question or suggestion you have?

   _____

   _____

   _____

◆ Write

Now, using the topic you've chosen, write your own paragraph. Review what you have learned in this chapter.

◆ After You Write

ACADEMIC POWER STRATEGY

Use a computer when you write. The computer makes writing easy. You can make changes in your drafts with the push of a button. You can revise and edit quickly and easily. The computer is useful in all classes and most useful in a writing class. If you don't have a computer, refer to Chapter 4 (the Learn About the Library section) to review where you can use computers on campus.

Apply the Strategy

Revise and edit your assignment for this chapter on a computer.

Revise

First, have someone look at the ideas in your writing. Give your finished paragraph to a classmate. Your classmate will complete these statements:

1. The writing is about this:

   _____

   _____

2. The writer says it is useful to read this because:

   _____

   _____

3. The writer describes these specific instructions, points, or events:

   _____

   _____

   _____

4. The writer could add or change this to improve the writing:

   _____

   _____

   _____

Using a computer, make changes to improve your writing.

Edit

Now have someone check your writing for organization and language. Give your revised paragraph to a classmate. Your classmate will answer these questions.

1. Does the first sentence explain why the reader should continue reading?   Yes   No

   If the answer is no, what can the writer add?

   _____

   _____

2. Does the writer use sequence words so that the writing is smooth?   Yes   No

   If the answer is no, what can the writer add?

   _____

   _____

3. Are there any language mistakes? (Please write them here.)
   Yes   No

   _____

   _____

   _____

Using a computer, make corrections to your writing.

PUTTING IT ALL TOGETHER

Use What You Have Learned

1. Write about similarities and differences between two kinds of cars, or compare the driving habits of two people, two states, or two countries.

2. Talk or write about a car of the future. Bring in a picture. Present it to the class.

Test-Taking Tip

Leave extra time at the end of an essay test to check the grammar, spelling, and punctuation of what you have written. Make any necessary corrections before you give your instructor the test. Sloppy grammar, spelling, and punctuation will usually result in a lower grade.

CHECK YOUR PROGRESS

On a scale of 1 to 5, rate how well you have mastered the goals set at the beginning of the chapter:

1 2 3 4 5 write instructions about how to drive or buy a car.

1 2 3 4 5 use diagrams to help you plan and organize your writing.

1 2 3 4 5 learn to anticipate reader questions in order to include important information in your writing.

1 2 3 4 5 use a computer when you write.

1 2 3 4 5 learn expressions of obligation.

If you've given yourself a 3 or lower on any of these goals:

- visit the *Tapestry* web site for additional practice.

- ask your instructor for extra help.

- review the sections of the chapter that you found difficult.

- work with a partner or study group to further your progress.

The Enneagram

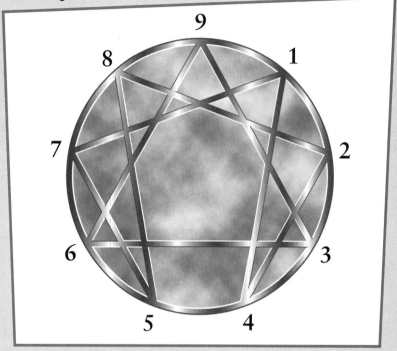

"When you know others, you're educated; when you know yourself, you're wise."

—Based on a quote from Lao-Tzu

How well do you know yourself? Choose three words that describe your personality and share them with a classmate.

THAT'S MY TYPE!

9

According to an ancient system of studying personalities, there are nine basic types of people. This system is called the *Enneagram* (pronounced ANY-a-gram). Experts believe the system began in the Middle East. A Russian teacher introduced it to Europe in the 1920s. It appeared in the United States in the 1960s. In this chapter, you will learn about the Enneagram system and think about your own personality type. You will also explore your relationships with others. At the end of the chapter, you will write about your natural skills and talents.

Setting Goals

In this chapter you will learn how to:

◈ write about your personality type.

In order to do this, you will:

◈ use reading selections as models for your writing.

◈ survey friends to collect information and ideas for your writing.

◈ learn to appreciate the differences among people in order to succeed in a diverse world.

◈ read two selections about personality types to prepare for writing.

◈ learn about word parts to expand your vocabulary for writing.

ACADEMIC POWER STRATEGY

Learn to appreciate the differences among people in order to succeed in a diverse world. In Chapter 5, you learned about cultural differences. But people are different in many ways. They come from big cities or small towns. Their parents are married or unmarried. They are members of different races, genders, or ethnic groups. When you appreciate all differences, you can be open to many experiences. Dealing effectively with differences is an important life skill.

Apply the Strategy

Follow these tips to deal effectively with diversity.

Tips for Dealing with Diversity

1. **Learn about different groups of people.** This will help you understand why people do the things they do. Read, watch movies, and talk to people to learn about their differences.

2. **Look for similarities.** It is easier to appreciate differences when you have something in common. Get to know people who seem different from you. You will discover that you are similar.

3. **Look at people as individuals.** Do not look at them as group representatives. When we see people as group members only, we do not see their unique and complex qualities. We *stereotype* when we do this. Avoid making general mistakes about people. Look at them as individuals.

Write short answers to these questions on another piece of paper.

1. Where do you find diversity in your life? At school? At work?

2. Explain how a group of people seem different from you. Find at least two things you have in common with them.

3. Write one thing you plan to do in order to deal effectively with diversity.

Getting Started

Think of three individuals in your family. How are you different from each of these people? Perhaps your mother makes decisions carefully and slowly. You make decisions quickly. Maybe your brother can repair anything that doesn't work. You don't like to fix things. Write some differences between you and people in your family. Then talk about the differences to a classmate.

SOME INFORMATION ABOUT A FAMILY MEMBER	SOME INFORMATION ABOUT ME: HOW I'M DIFFERENT
Name: _____	_____
_____	_____
_____	_____
Name: _____	_____
_____	_____
_____	_____
Name: _____	_____
_____	_____
_____	_____

MEETING THE TOPIC

Talk with a partner about the illustration. The picture shows nine types of people in a classroom. On the following pages, match the descriptions of the people to what they are saying.

One's *personality* is his or her habits, attitudes, traits, and moods. It is the total effect of a person.

One: Perfectionists like to be right. They have high goals. They try to do everything perfectly.

Two: Helpers are friendly and caring. They try to help people.

Three: Achievers are ambitious. They try to be productive and achieve success.

Four: Romantics are sensitive and expressive. They try to understand their feelings.

Five: Observers like to know a lot of things. They try not to look foolish.

Six: Questioners are loyal and responsible. They try to find security.

Seven: Adventurers are energetic and optimistic. They try to make a difference in the world.

Eight: Asserters are direct and confident. They try not to be dependent.

Nine: Peacemakers are cheerful and supportive. They try to avoid conflict.

There are many systems that study and explain human personality. The Myers-Briggs system looks at our preferences when we are born. The Enneagram looks at how we learn to live in the world.

The Classroom

a. _____ It's great that Tazu isn't unhappy today. I hope Jean-Paul feels better about his girlfriend!

b. _____ I have to leave immediately after class. I have so much work to do.

c. _____ I've gotten a perfect score on every quiz. I plan to continue this class without making a mistake.

d. _____ Who needs a pencil? Does anyone need to use my dictionary?

e. _____ Why isn't Lola in class today? Doesn't she like us?

f. _____ Here's my plan: I'll finish my homework after class, volunteer at the library, then recycle all our bottles, cans, and newspapers. I know I can get it all done!

g. _____ Please show me the answers to the homework questions, though I'm sure I got them all right. I want to know what tonight's homework assignment will be. Pass me the dictionary!

h. _____ I'm glad everyone else is answering the teacher's questions. I always learn something when I listen.

i. _____ This class is so wonderful. I love my classmates and really admire my teacher. I will never forget this great experience.

Freewrite

Freewrite about yourself. Do you match one of the people in the classroom? Maybe you are a combination of different people. Answer any of these questions to begin. Then write some other things about your personality.

- Are your friends and their opinions very important to you?

- Is it easy for you to work hard and focus on your goals?

- Do you like to spend time alone or with other people?

- Is it important for you to do things 'perfectly'?

Write for at least ten minutes. You will develop this subject later for the writing assignment.

TUNING IN: "Type D Personality"

© CNN

This video is about a study that suggests a new personality type. Listen for the signs of a Type D personality. Pay attention to what can happen to people with this personality type. Watch the video, then answer the questions.

1. A person with a Type A personality

   a. is busy, hurried, and stressed.

   b. has lots of kids.

   c. is healthy.

2. What does Type D stand for?

   a. depressed

   b. distressed

   c. dressed up

> **I have a fear of being disliked, even by people I dislike.**
>
> **—OPRAH WINFREY**

3. People with Type D personalities are often

    a. insecure.

    b. socially inhibited.

    c. both of these.

4. Why is it important to know your personality type?

    a. Your personality can affect your health.

    b. Your health can affect your personality.

    c. Treatment can make a difference.

5. What are the "keys" to a healthy life?

    a. avoiding a repeat heart attack

    b. staying busy

    c. low stress and a positive outlook

6. *Challenge Question:* Which personality type on the Enneagram is closest to Type D?

EXPANDING YOUR LANGUAGE

Vocabulary Check

The following words and expressions will help you with the reading and writing in this chapter. Check the ones that you know. Learn the definitions of new words and add them to the Vocabulary Section of your Writer's Portfolio.

_____ basic	_____ judgmental
_____ be based on	_____ natural
_____ combination	_____ point of view
_____ complete	_____ preference
_____ complex	_____ similarities
_____ deal with something	_____ stick to something
_____ get along with someone	_____ system
_____ have something in common with someone else	

Vocabulary Building

1. Match these words and expressions from the Vocabulary Check in Column 1 to words with the **opposite** meaning in Column 2.

Column 1	Column 2
similarities	artificial
get along with someone	begin
complete	simple
complex	dislike someone
natural	differences

2. Complete the paragraph by using words and expressions from the Vocabulary Check. Choose from this list:

natural	preference	similarities	complex
stick to	get along with	system	deal with
is based on	having something in common with someone else		
point of view			

"Birds of a feather flock together." This is an English proverb. It means that people have a (a) _____ to make friends with others who are like them. It's (b) _____ to choose friends with (c) _____. Take me, for example. I (d) _____ with people who are very serious about their work. They set goals and (e) _____ those goals. When they have problems at work, they don't run away from the problems. My friends (f)_____ their problems. I'm serious too. I have to be serious. I work for a huge computer company. I manage a (g) _____ (h) _____ of circuit boards. All my friends appreciate my (i) _____ about work. Of course they do. Friendship, after all, (j) _____ (k) _____.

3. You have learned new vocabulary from nine chapters about many different topics. This is a good time to review the Vocabulary Section of your Writer's Portfolio. Study the words and expressions you still find difficult. How many new words and expressions have you learned?

   a. 40–60

   b. 60–80

   c. 80–100

READING FOR WRITING

LANGUAGE LEARNING STRATEGY

Use reading selections as models for your writing. Most writers read a lot. They get ideas from reading, and they learn ways of presenting and organizing ideas. Using reading selections as models for writing will help you expand your skills.

Apply the Strategy

You will read two selections about the Enneagram. Use these articles to help you with your writing in this chapter.

Reading 1 explains where the Enneagram came from and how it can be helpful. Before you read, talk to a classmate and answer these questions:

• We all have unique personalities. Where do we get them?

• Can a person change his or her personality?

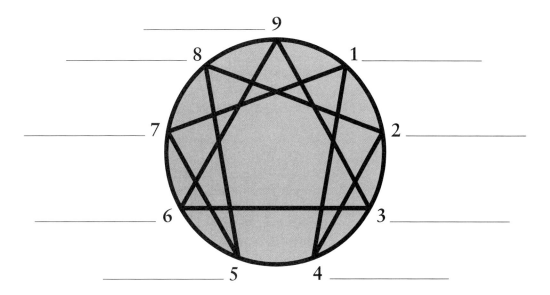

Reading 1: The Enneagram

The Enneagram is a **system** of nine personality types. The name comes from *Ennea,* which is Greek for the number nine, and *gram,* which means something drawn or written. A circle with nine points represents the Enneagram. The Enneagram **is based on** the belief that early in life people develop strategies for **getting along with** others and solving problems. These strategies come from our **natural** talents and abilities. When we study the Enneagram, we learn more about the strategies we use. We get to know ourselves and others better, and we understand attitudes and behaviors from many different points of view. We feel better about ourselves and less **judgmental** about others. The Enneagram is a **complex system** of understanding different types of people, but a simple introduction to it can improve the way you live your life and get along with other people.

—Renee Baron and Elizabeth Wagele

1. What are three things the Enneagram can help you do?

   a. _____

   b. _____

   c. _____

2. Look at the Enneagram diagram. There is a line next to each number. Write the "type name" that matches each number. Refer to Meeting the Topic on page 166.

3. Which information is **not** included in the reading selection "The Enneagram"?

    a. the meaning of the name

    b. the names of the nine personality types

    c. when the Enneagram became popular in Europe

    d. what the Enneagram teaches us

    e. the difference between the Enneagram and learning styles

    f. why the Enneagram is represented by a circle

4. Write a short letter to someone you know. Explain what you have learned about the Enneagram.

Dear ————————,

_____

_____

_____

_____

_____

Sincerely,

————————————

Reading 2 is a description of the nine personality types of the Enneagram. Before you read, talk to a classmate and answer these questions:

- Have you ever studied personality types? Learning styles? Astrological signs? Sun or shadow traits? If so, what did you learn?

- Based on what you've learned so far, what "type" on the Enneagram do you think you are? Why?

Reading 2: The Nine Types of the Enneagram

Name	Common Careers	Favorite Free-Time Activities	How to Get Along with Them	Some Suggestions for This Type
1. The Perfectionist	Dentists Doctors Police officers Mechanics	Doing community service Exercising Studying	Help them laugh at themselves. Don't give them all the work. Recognize their strengths.	Take time to enjoy yourself. Tell jokes and read cartoons. Learn how to reduce stress.

Name	Common Careers	Favorite Free-Time Activities	How to Get Along with Them	Some Suggestions for This Type
2. The Helper	Salespeople Secretaries Teachers Health professionals	Getting together with friends and family Caring for children Gardening Reading	Tell them you like them. Have fun times together. Be gentle and kind.	Focus on yourself. Be kind to yourself. Don't "overgive" to others.
3. The Achiever	Businesspeople Lawyers Bankers Politicians Performers	Working on hobbies or projects Exercising Volunteering to help others	Leave them alone to work. Don't be too negative. Help them keep their environment full of harmony and peace.	Take time to relax. Take a vacation. Choose work that you love.
4. The Romantic	Musicians Artists Dancers Psychologists	Spending time with friends and family Going to concerts Shopping	Give them compliments. Respect their talents. Be a good friend.	Be proud of your skills and talents. Learn self-discipline. Be kind to yourself.
5. The Observer	Scientists Technicians Musicians Artists Writers	Reading books Having discussions Going to museums Playing difficult games	Don't be dependent on them. Give them time to think. Don't be too emotional.	Take risks and speak up. Listen to others when they speak. Learn to express your feelings
6. The Questioner	Military carrers Corporate workers Educators	Getting physical exercise Enjoying nature activities Being active	Be clear and direct. Don't judge them. Reassure them. Laugh and make jokes.	Spend time with trustworthy people. Believe the positive things people say about you. Learn that it is OK to make mistakes.
7. The Adventurer	Pilots Tour guides Translators Outdoor jobs Teachers Nurses	Trying thrilling sports Traveling Playing games Going to concerts, movies Learning new things	Don't tell them what to do. Accept them as they are. Give them affection and freedom.	Take care of your health. See the negative with the positive. Be a good listener. Accept that others are slower than you.
8. The Asserter	Business leaders Athletes Lawyers Entrepreneurs	Doing outdoor activities Playing difficult sports Having high-energy fun	Don't be afraid of their anger. Let them be alone.	Be aware that your directness may be difficult for some people. Express your appreciation often. Learn to compromise.
9. The Peacemaker	Diplomats Helping professions	Flexible Like all activities	Listen and don't judge. Don't fight. Show physical affection.	Change a situation that isn't right; don't wait for it to change. Set goals; make a timeline. Express your opinions.

1. Which Ennegram types:

    a. have lots of energy and like to stay busy?

    _____

    b. should learn stress reduction?

    _____

    c. need support and encouragement?

    _____

    d. like to spend time alone?

    _____

2. Match these adjectives to the personality types.

    _____ cheerful   a. perfectionists

    _____ energetic   b. helpers

    _____ expressive   c. achievers

    _____ loyal   d. romantics

    _____ ambitious   e. observers

    _____ knowledgeable   f. questioners

    _____ caring   g. adventurers

    _____ productive   h. asserters

    _____ well-organized   i. peacemakers

3. Can you identify your personality type? Answer these questions to find your type. (Do this exercise alone. Don't tell your class-mates. They will try to guess your personality type in the next exercise.)

    a. What are three adjectives that describe you?

    _____

    b. How do you like to spend your free time?

    _____

    c. What profession do you have now or do you want to have?

    _____

    d. Which personality type do you match most closely?

    _____

4. Try to identify the personality types of three people in your class. Begin by completing the chart with information about classmates

you know well. Then read your writing to the class. See if your classmates agree.

(Name of student) _____ is (three adjectives that describe this person)_____, _____, and _____. S/he likes to spend time (favorite free-time activity) _____. S/he is/will be a good (name of profession) _____. Therefore, I believe (name of student) _____ is a(n) (personality type) _____.

Grammar You Can Use: Word Parts

Learning word parts and how to use them will expand your vocabulary for writing. There are three parts: stems, prefixes, and suffixes.

- Prefixes and suffixes are connected to **stems,** the basic part of the word.
- **Prefixes** come at the beginning of words. They affect the meaning of a word.
- **Suffixes** come at the end of words. They affect the part of speech.

Study some common prefixes and suffixes in the following charts:

Prefixes	Meaning	Example
re-	again	**re**state
inter-	between	**inter**action
multi-	many	**multi**cultural
un-	not	**un**happy
mis-	wrong	**mis**take
vis-	see, sight	**vis**ualize

Suffixes	Meaning (Part of Speech)	Example
-er	one who (noun)	teach**er**
-istic	in this way (adverb)	real**istic**
-ful	full of (adjective)	peace**ful**
-al	related to (adjective)	music**al**
-ist	one who is (noun)	scient**ist**

How many words can you create? How many words can you remember? Review information from this chapter and all of the chapters you've completed. Create as many words as possible.

1. Start with these prefixes. Add stems and/or suffixes. Work in teams.

   re- _____   multi- _____   mis- _____

   inter- _____   un- _____   vis- _____

2. Start with these stems. Add suffixes. Work in teams.

   perfection _____   help _____   art _____

   dance _____   shop _____   bank _____

   observe _____   achieve _____   teach _____

   color _____   emotion _____   perform _____

   direct _____   work _____   play _____

3. Now write a paragraph about your personality based on one of the Enneagram types. Use the freewrite you began in Meeting the Topic and include new words from this chapter.

   _____

   _____

   _____

   _____

   _____

   _____

   _____

   _____

FROM READING TO WRITING

◆ **Getting Ready to Write**   **Choose a Topic**

You are going to write a paragraph about your personality type. Describe your personality in one or more of the following ways:

- Explain how you are one type according to the Enneagram System.
- Explain how you are a combination of types according to the Enneagram system.

Here are some instructions for writing:

Instructions for Writing About Your Personality Type

1. Begin by **telling the reader about the Enneagram system.** Here is an example from this chapter:

   • *The Enneagram is a system of nine personality types.*

2. The purpose of your writing is to tell your reader about your personality type. Organize your writing in one of two ways:

   • One way is to **announce your personality type first** and **give examples** to show how you match this type. This way is common in academic writing.

   • Another way is to **give specific examples first and then present your personality type.** This way is more dramatic.

   Choose the way you like best. Or try both ways and choose the writing that is easiest to understand.

3. **Include two kinds of examples** of personality types:

   • Use **general examples** that describe what all people of the same type do or think or feel.

   • Use **specific examples** of your actions, thoughts, or feelings to show how you match a specific personality type.

LANGUAGE LEARNING STRATEGY

Apply the Strategy

Survey friends to collect information and ideas for your writing. Your friends and classmates can help you gather information. Use them as resources. Ask them to answer your questions, share their experiences, and give their opinions.

Gather information about the personality types of three people who are not in your class. The information from the survey will help you collect examples for your writing. Use the questions from Reading for Writing for persons 1, 2, and 3. Show the Enneagram to your friends if you like.

It is common to be asked questions about your personality in job interviews.

Which Type Are You?

a. What are three adjectives that describe you?

_____

_____

b. How do you like to spend your free time?

_____

_____

c. What profession do you have now or do you want to have?

_____

_____

d. Which personality type do you match?

_____

_____

Study an Example

Before you write, read this paragraph written by a college student.

Just My Type

The Enneagram, a way of describing nine different types of people, changed my life. I became proud and even confident when I learned about the Enneagram. This system said it was OK to be who I am. I love to be with people. I like to have dinner parties and invite different friends and introduce them to each other. I love to do things for people I love. I work in my sister's garden, help my friends paint their house, and cook for my partner's business meetings. I love it when people appreciate me. I'm learning to appreciate myself. I'm so happy to discover I'm a Type 4, a real Romantic, on the Enneagram chart!

1. What examples does the writer use to show her personality type?

   a. _____

   b. _____

   c. _____

2. What is one thing you noticed and liked about the writing?

   _____

3. What is one question or suggestion you have?

   _____

◇ Write

Now write about your personality type. Use the writing you've already begun in the chapter.

◇ After You Write

Revise

First, have someone look at the ideas in your writing. Give your finished paragraph to a classmate. Your classmate will complete these statements.

1. The writing is about this personality type: _____

2. These are ways the person matches this type:

   a. _____

   b. _____

3. The writer could add or change this to improve the writing:

   _____

   _____

Make changes to improve your writing.

Edit

Now have someone check your writing for organization and language. Give your revised paragraph to a classmate. Your classmate will answer the following questions:

1. Does the first sentence describe the Enneagram? Yes No

2. Does the writing follow one of the ways to organize ideas in Instructions for Writing About Your Personality Type?
Yes No

3. Do you like the way the writer organizes his or her ideas? Explain.

_____

_____

4. Does the writer use prefixes and suffixes correctly?
Yes No

If the answer is no, which words should be corrected?

_____

_____

5. Are there any language mistakes? (Please write them here.)
Yes No

_____

_____

Make corrections to your writing.

PUTTING IT ALL TOGETHER

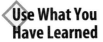

Use What You Have Learned

1. Interview someone outside of class about his or her personality type. Present the results of your interview to the class.

2. If you are interested in this topic, read more about individual preferences. Look for information on learning styles and multiple intelligences. Present what you learn to the class.

Test-Taking Tip

Study tests after they are returned to you to learn from your mistakes. Try to understand the reason for mistakes you made on the test. Did you have trouble understanding the directions? Did you misread the question? Did you not study hard enough? Work to make sure you don't make the same mistake on future tests.

CHECK YOUR PROGRESS

On a scale of 1 to 5, rate how well you have mastered the goals set at the beginning of the chapter:

1 2 3 4 5   write about your personality type.

1 2 3 4 5   use reading selections as models for your writing.

1 2 3 4 5   survey friends to collect information and ideas for your writing.

1 2 3 4 5   learn to appreciate the differences among people in order to succeed in a diverse world.

1 2 3 4 5   learn about word parts to expand your vocabulary for writing.

If you've given yourself a 3 or lower on any of these goals:

- visit the *Tapestry* web site for additional practice.
- ask your instructor for extra help.
- review the sections of the chapter that you found difficult.
- work with a partner or study group to further your progress.

"Genius is 1% inspiration and 99% perspiration."

—Thomas Edison

This is a photo of Thomas Edison, the inventor of the electric light and the phonograph. Some people say he was the greatest inventor in history. Do you agree? What other important inventions can you name?

10

UNINTENTIONAL INVENTIONS

Have you heard the saying "We learn from our mistakes"? How about "We live with our mistakes"? In this chapter you will read and write about inventions. None of the inventions were planned. You will learn how people made these "accidental discoveries" and how the inventions make our lives easier and more fun. After reading and thinking about inventions, you will write about an invention of your own.

Setting Goals

In this chapter you will learn how to:

◈ write at least two paragraphs about an invention.

In order to do this, you will:

◈ practice getting new ideas _____ ones

◈ learn new words in "famili_____

◈ reflect on what you've le_____ accomplishments.

◈ read two selections abou_____

◈ practice using verbs in t_____

[handwritten note:] http://web2.uvcs.uvic.cal/ck/Sample/intermediate/map.htm

[handwritten note:] Intermediate Writing course

3

◆**Getting Started**

Think of some inventions that you find funny, important, or useful. What do they do? How do they help you? Begin with the inventions below. Write your ideas about inventions in the chart; then talk about them with a classmate.

Invention	What It Does	How It Helps Me
paper towel	*dries, cleans*	*I can use it to clean and then throw it away.*
disposable camera	*takes photos*	*I don't have to own an expensive camera to take photos.*

MEETING THE TOPIC

◆**Talk with a Partner**

Discuss the inventions in the following photos. Each of them was invented by mistake. Describe what they are; then answer the questions.

a.

b.

c.

d.

e.

How do you think they were invented?

Velcro was invented by George de Mestral, a Swiss engineer who came back from a walk with small rough-edged plants on this clothing. He studied the plants (called burrs) and invented "hook-and-loop fasteners" in 1948. It has thousands of uses today.

a. ice cream cone

_____

b. guide dogs for blind people

_____

c. Frisbee

_____

d. tea

_____

e. Velcro

_____

 Freewrite

Tea was discovered by Shen Nung, a Chinese emperor, in 2737 B.C. He was boiling water, and some leaves fell in the hot water. It smelled good, and he tasted it. Today, tea is the most popular drink in the world.

Freewrite about an invention that you find useful and interesting. Answer any of these questions to begin. Then write some other things you know or want to know about this invention.

- What is the invention?
- Why does it interest you?
- When was it invented?
- Who invented it?
- How does it help you?

This is the beginning of your writing assignment for this chapter. You will develop your freewrite through exercises and ideas from reading selections.

TUNING IN: "High-Tech Gadgets"

© CNN

The video you'll watch here shows some new inventions at a high-tech show. As you watch the video, think about how these inventions make life more convenient or more fun. Try to answer all the questions correctly after the first viewing.

1. Which inventions or gadgets were **not** at this high-tech show?

   a. cell phones

   b. mini-computers

   c. family radios

> Frisbees began as metal pie pans. Students at Yale University threw the pie pans to each other after eating the pies. In the 1950s, Frisbees were made in plastic, and Frisbee games became a popular sport.

> Name the greatest of all inventors. Accident.
>
> —MARK TWAIN

2. How much does the digital still camera cost?

   a. $250–$300

   b. $400–$450

   c. $1400–$1450

3. What is new about all these gadgets?

   a. They're smaller and lighter.

   b. They're better quality than previous gadgets.

   c. Both of these.

4. What is a key word in electronics?

   a. *smaller*

   b. *lighter*

   c. *wireless*

5. What does "all this stuff will be less next year" mean?

   a. There will be fewer gadgets.

   b. The gadgets will cost less money.

   c. There will be fewer people to sell gadgets.

6. Which gadget do you want to buy? Why?

   _____

   _____

7. *Challenge Question:* What high-tech invention will be popular **next** year?

   _____

   _____

LANGUAGE LEARNING STRATEGY

Get new ideas from old ones to present original thoughts in your writing. Good writers introduce fresh, new ideas. Where do they find these ideas? Sometimes, new ideas come from old ones. When you want to write about a future invention, think about a past invention that could be made better with a few changes. Use what you already know to think of new ideas.

Apply the Strategy

Take the familiar objects in the list below to design newer, more useful objects. Use your imagination. Study the example first. Add one familiar object in the last row. When you are finished, share your new ideas with your classmates.

FAMILIAR OBJECT	WHAT IT DOES NOW	WHAT IT WILL BE	WHAT IT WILL DO
ballpoint pen	writes	no-mistake pen	corrects mistakes as it writes
backpack			
car			
personal computer			

EXPANDING YOUR LANGUAGE

◇Vocabulary Check

These words and expressions will help you with the reading and writing in this chapter. Check the words you already know. Study the definitions of new words and add them to the Vocabulary Section of your Writer's Portfolio.

_____ become an instant success

_____ by accident

_____ by mistake

_____ come about

_____ discover

_____ do/try an experiment

_____ help someone do something

_____ on purpose

_____ replace

_____ run out of

_____ train an animal/person to do something

_____ unintentional

◆Vocabulary Building

Serendipity is the ability to see something valuable that you weren't looking for.

1. Match the words and expressions in Column 1 to those with the same meaning in Column 2.

Column 1	Column 2
train	find
discover	intentional
come about	unintentional
run out of	teach
by accident	take the place
replace	not have enough
on purpose	happen

2. Complete the sentences in the following paragraph. Use each of these words and expressions once.

discover	by mistake	invention	tried an experiment
ran out of	by accident	came about	successful
discovered	helped	accidentally	

Some of the most useful discoveries (a) _____ (b) _____. For example, the (c) _____ of the rubber tire happened (d) _____. Rubber had many uses from ancient times to the 1800s. However, in the early nineteenth century, people wanted to (e) _____ more ways to use rubber. In the 1830s, an American named Charles Goodyear (f) _____ by mixing rubber with many other things to make it more useful. He was not (g) _____, and he almost (h) _____ ideas. Then one day in 1839, he dropped some rubber on a hot stove (i) _____. When he began to clean it up, he (j) _____ that the heat (k) _____ the rubber be firm and flexible. Because of Goodyear's mistake, rubber now has many uses. Rubber is used for medical supplies, the bottoms of shoes, thousands of children's toys, and tires for cars, trucks, bicycles, wagons, and motorcycles. In fact, rubber is one of the world's most successful industries today. Goodyear's mistake was a lucky accident.

LANGUAGE LEARNING STRATEGY

L earn new words in "families" to expand your vocabulary for writing. In Chapter 5, you learned that some words can be more than one part of speech. In Chapter 9, you connected prefixes and suffixes to stems to create words. Words with the same stem and related meanings make up a *word* **family.** When you learn new words, learn as many members of the word family as you can.

graph   tele**graph**   **graphic**   holo**graph**   picto**graph**

Apply the Strategy

Read the words below. Put the words in "families," or groups with the same stem by placing them on the same line in the correct box. Look at the example. Add one more word family if you can.

invent   discover   successfully   instantly   replacement   success

instant   inventor   discovery   improvement   creative

imaginative   successful   improve   imagination   invention

create   imagine   replace   creativity

Word Family	Noun (person)	Noun (thing)	Adverb	Verb	Adjective
1	inventor	invention	inventively	invent	inventive
2					
3					
4					
5					
6					
7					
8					

READING FOR WRITING

You will read two selections about inventions that happened by mistake.

Reading 1 is about the invention of the ice cream cone. Before you read, answer these questions:

- How often do you eat ice cream cones?

- What is your favorite flavor of ice cream?

- On pages 184 and 185, in Meeting the Topic, you made some guesses about the invention of the ice cream cone. What were they?

Reading 1: "I Scream" for a Cone

1   What would ice cream be without ice cream cones? Although most people know what ice cream cones are and even eat them often, they probably do not know how they were invented. And they probably do not know that they were invented by two people from different parts of the world at about the same time. And both inventors were immigrants living in America.

2   The first inventor was a **street vendor**[1] from Syria. Ernest A. Hamwi made and sold *zalabia,* a thin, sweet waffle. He worked at the **World's Fair**[2] in St. Louis, Missouri during the summer of 1904. Another vendor was selling ice cream nearby. Summers in St.

[1]**street vendor:** a person who sell things from a temporary location, often on the street

[2]**World's Fair:** an international exposition that takes place in cities all over the world

Louis are hot, so the ice cream was selling fast and soon the vendor **ran out of** plates for the ice cream. Hamwi noticed this. He quickly rolled his zalabia into a cone, an object which is closed on the bottom and open at the top. He handed the cone to the ice cream vendor to hold the ice cream, and ice cream cones **became an instant success.**

3   At about the same time, an Italian living in New York invented a better way to serve lemon ice in paper cones. Italo Marchiony sold refreshments from his pushcart. When he found that paper cones were weak and messy, he **replaced** them with pastry cones. His business improved instantly—customers could eat the containers as well as the ice cream!

—Charlotte Folts Jones

Scoop of ice cream

cone

1. Are these sentences true or false? If false, write a new sentence with the correct information.

   a. The ice cream cone was invented in North America by a person born in North America.

   _____

   b. Both Hamwi and Marchiony were vendors at the 1904 World's Fair in St. Louis, Missouri.

   _____

   c. The ice cream cone is about 200 years old.

   _____

2. Complete the following with information from the reading:

   What is the name of the invention? _____

   What does it look like? _____

   What does it do? _____

   How does it improve life? _____

More than 6,500 people in the United States use guide dogs.

Reading 2 is about the discovery of the use of dogs as guides for blind people. Before you read, talk to a classmate and answer these questions:

- Have you seen a guide dog walking with a blind person?
- Do guide dogs help blind people in your native culture?
- What might be difficult about having a guide dog?
- What were your guesses about how the idea of guide dogs came about? Refer to Meeting the Topic on pages 184–185.

Reading 2: Guide Dogs

1   At the end of World War I, a German doctor, his dog, and one of the doctor's patients were walking out of a hospital. The patient was blind from **wounds**[1] in the war. The doctor went back into the hospital and left the dog and the patient alone. When the doctor came out a second time, the dog and the patient were gone. Where did they go? How did they find their way?

2   The doctor learned that the dog **helped the blind patient find his way** across the hospital **grounds.**[2] He thought it was amazing that a dog could guide a blind person safely. He decided to **try an experiment** and **train dogs to lead blind people.** When he found that trained dogs could guide blind people successfully, he proposed a guide dog program to the German government. About ten years later, an American woman visited the guide dog training program in Germany and wrote about it in an American magazine. Today there are ten large companies that **train** dogs and teach blind people how to use them. Guide dogs have helped blind people lead happier and more independent lives.

—Charlotte Folts Jones

[1]**wounds:** injuries

[2]**grounds:** area around a building or group of buildings

1. Draw a picture or story map showing where the doctor, the patient, and the dog went. Retell the story to a classmate and use your story map.

How Guide Dogs Were Invented: Story Map

2. Complete the following with information from the reading:

   What is the name of the invention? _____

   What does it look like? _____

   What does it do? _____

   What are it's benefits? _____

3. This exercise has two parts. First, underline the sentences in the reading selection that contain the following expressions:

   to try an experiment   *to teach someone to learn something*

   to think it is amazing   *to train an animal to do something*

Now, complete these sentences by using these expressions. Write about your own experiences.

a. I trained an animal to _____ when

_____

_____ .

b. I taught (a person) _____ to learn

_____ when _____

_____

_____ .

c. I tried an experiment when _____

_____

_____ .

d. I thought it was amazing when _____

_____

_____ .

Grammar You Can Use: Passive Voice

It is useful to use the passive voice when writing about inventions.

- A verb is in the **active** voice if the subject is doing the action of the sentence.

  *Eleven-year-old Shahid Minapara **invented** a nightlight.*

- A verb is in the **passive voice** if the subject is receiving the action of the sentence.

  *The light **is attached** to a person's hand.*

Form the passive voice by using the correct form of *to be* with the **past participle** of the verb.

*Shahid's nightlights **are used** by children and adults.*

Practice forming the passive by completing the following sentences. Be careful to conjugate the verb *to be* and put it in the correct tense.

Intentional Inventions (by Kids)

Kids are sometimes the best inventors. Fifteen-year old Krysta Morlan invented a cast cooler. (A cast is a plaster covering to keep an injured body part from moving.) The cast cooler is for people who (expect)

(1) _____ to wear casts for broken bones. The cast cooler (power) (2) _____ by a small battery. It (design) (3) _____ to relieve people of the itching they experience as they heal. Krysta (awarded) (4) _____ a prize for her invention. She (honor) (5) _____ by Lemelson–MIT at a recent ceremony. The Lemelson–MIT program (establish) (6) _____ to encourage inventors. Inventors aren't always adults!

FROM READING TO WRITING

Getting Ready to Write

Choose a Topic

Write at least two paragraphs about an invention. Choose one of the following topics:

- Write about an invention that you find useful and interesting. Describe what it is, what it does, and how it makes your life easier or more fun. If you don't know about its discovery, make some guesses.

- Invent something and write about it. Describe what it is, what it will do, and how it will make your life easier or more fun.

- Write about an inventor who discovered something important either by accident or on purpose. Include some information about the inventor, but the most important part of your paper is about the invention or inventions.

Here are some instructions for writing:

Instructions for Writing About an Invention

1. Describe the invention so that the reader knows what it looks like. Here is an example from this chapter:
   - *Hamwi rolled his zalabia into a cone, an object which is closed on the bottom and open at the top.*

2. Write about what the invention does. Here is an example from this chapter:
   - *Rubber is used for medical supplies, the bottoms of shoes, thousands of children's toys, and tires for cars, trucks, bicycles, wagons, and motorcycles.*

3. Show how the invention makes life easier or more fun. Look at this example:

  - *Guide dogs have helped blind people lead happier and more independent lives.*

4. Make sure that you write about only one important idea or topic in each paragraph. The following example paragraph describes only Marchiony's discovery of the ice cream cone:

  - *At about the same time, an Italian living in New York invented a better way to serve lemon ice in paper cones. Italo Marchiony sold refreshments from his pushcart. When he found that paper cones were weak and messy, he replaced them with pastry cones. His business improved instantly—customers could eat the containers as well as the ice cream!*

Study an Example

Before you write, read this paragraph.

Twenty-First Century Diapers

Pampers! Huggies! Greet your competition for the 21st century: diapers that change color! These new diapers look like normal diapers, but they are made with magical ingredients that will make your life with babies easier and less expensive. You won't have to check your baby's diaper every hour. Instead, when the diaper is wet, it will change color so that you will know it is time to change. Like litmus paper, the material of the disposable diaper is sensitive to moisture. When wet, the diaper will change from white to pink (for girl diapers) and from white to blue (for boy diapers). No more wasting dry diapers. And no more babies with wet diapers for several hours because you didn't know the diaper was wet. We will have happy babies and happy parents.

1. This invention would be interesting to these people:

   a. adolescents.

   b. parents.

   c. both of these.

2. What is new or different about these diapers?

   a. They are disposable.

   b. They change color when wet.

   c. They are for babies.

3. The writer explains

   a. what the invention looks like.

   b. how the invention makes life easier or more fun.

   c. how the invention works.

4. What is one question or suggestion you have for this writer?

   _____

   _____

Write

Now write two paragraphs about the topic you chose on page 195. Review what you have learned in this chapter. Use the writing you have already done.

After You Write

Revise

First, have someone look at the ideas in your writing. Give your finished paragraphs to a classmate. Your classmate will complete these statements:

1. The paragraphs are about this invention:

   _____

2. This is what the invention looks like:

   _____

   _____

3. This is what the invention does:

   _____

   _____

4. This is how the invention makes life easier or more fun:

_____

_____

5. The writer could add or change this to improve the paragraphs:

_____

_____

Make changes to improve your writing.

Edit

Now have someone check your paragraphs for organization and language. Give your revised writing to a classmate. Your classmate will answer these questions:

1. Is the writing in each paragraph about one important idea?
   Yes   No

   If the answer is no, which sentences should the writer add or omit?

   _____

   _____

2. Does the writer use the passive voice correctly?   Yes   No

   If the answer is no, which words or expressions should the writer correct?

   _____

3. Did you find language mistakes? (Please write them here.)
   Yes   No

   _____

   _____

4. Do you have any suggestions for improving the organization or correctness of this assignment?   Yes   No

   _____

   _____

Make corrections to your writing.

PUTTING IT ALL TOGETHER

◇ **Use What You Have Learned**

1. Read about another invention that interests you. Write about it. Read your writing to the class.

2. Draw, build, or describe your own invention. Make a presentation in class.

3. Pretend you are a famous inventor. Come to class dressed as this person. Talk about your discovery and how it happened.

ACADEMIC POWER STRATEGY

Apply the Strategy

Reflect on what you've learned so that you can recognize your accomplishments. It is important to review your work regularly. This way, you see what you have learned and are reminded of your progress.

1. Review your Writer's Portfolio now. Look for writing assignments for each of the categories below, and complete the chart.

	Title of Assignment and Date
Which was your favorite piece of writing? Why?	
Which writing assignment got the best grade? Why?	
Which writing assignment was the most difficult? Why?	
Which piece of writing shows the most progress? Why?	

2. On the last page of your Writer's Portfolio, write a short letter of reflection about your work for this class. Include notes from the chart above. Use this frame to get started, and add some of your own ideas.

(continued on next page)

Dear Reader,

This is my completed Writer's Portfolio for (course title)

_____ (semester or beginning and end dates of

course) _____. I want to tell you about my writ-

ing now. Here is what I learned to do well:_____,

_____, and _____. Here's

what I really enjoyed: _____, _____,

and _____. I still want to improve _____

and _____. I want to add this: _____

_____.

                           Sincerely,

               (Your name) _____

Keep this portfolio. You may show it to a teacher or keep it to review for future classes. It is a record of your progress.

Test-Taking Tip

Meet with your instructor to discuss your test after it is returned to you. Ask your
instructor what he or she thought of your test results. Ask what areas the instructor
feels you need to work on. Listen carefully to their advice and you will know what
you need to improve in order to do well on future tests.

CHECK YOUR PROGRESS

On a scale of 1 to 5, rate how well you have mastered the goals set
at the beginning of the chapter:

1 2 3 4 5   write at least two paragraphs about an invention.

1 2 3 4 5   practice getting new ideas from old ones.

1 2 3 4 5   learn new words in "families."

1 2 3 4 5   reflect on what you've learned.

1 2 3 4 5   practice using verbs in the passive voice.

If you've given yourself a 3 or lower on any of these goals:

- visit the *Tapestry* web site for additional practice.
- ask your instructor for extra help.
- review the sections of the chapter that you found difficult.
- work with a partner or study group to further your progress.

SKILLS INDEX

PHOTO CREDITS

Photos, with the exception of some or all on the following pages, were taken by Jonathan Stark, Heinle & Heinle, for the Image Resource Bank:

p. 2, provided by Meredith Pike-Baky; p. 5, Corbis; p. 9, provided by Meredith Pike-Baky; p. 17, Super Stock; p. 22, provided by Meredith Pike-Baky; p. 25, Corbis and provided by Meredith Pike-Baky; p. 28, Corbis; p. 34, Corbis; p. 36, Corbis; p. 40, provided by Meredith Pike-Baky; p. 42 Super Stock and Corbis; p. 43, provided by Meredith Pike-Baky; p. 49, Super Stock and Corbis; p. 53, provided by Meredith Pike-Baky; p. 56, Corbis; p. 60, provided by Meredith Pike-Baky; p. 70, Corbis; p. 72, provided by Meredith Pike-Baky; p. 76, Corbis; p. 80, provided by Meredith Pike-Baky; p. 83, provided by Meredith Pike-Baky and Corbis; p. 87, Corbis; p. 89, provided by Meredith Pike-Baky; p. 92, provided by Meredith Pike-Baky; p. 97, Corbis; p. 108, provided by Meredith Pike-Baky; p. 110, Corbis; p. 111, provided by Meredith Pike-Baky; p. 112, provided by Meredith Pike-Baky; p. 117, Corbis; p. 118, Corbis; p. 124, Corbis; p. 127, Corbis; p. 129, provided by Meredith Pike-Baky; p. 142, Super Stock; p. 144, Corbis; p. 145, Corbis and Super Stock; p. 147, Super Stock; p. 149, Corbis; p. 153, Corbis; p. 156, provided by Meredith Pike-Baky; p. 157, Super Stock; p. 177, Corbis; p. 182, Corbis; p. 184 Corbis; p. 187, Corbis; p. 190, Corbis; p. 191, Corbis; p. 193, Corbis; p. 196, Corbis.